where

are

we

going

so

fast?

finding the sacred in everyday moments

Jim Warda

Foreword by Jack Canfield

SHEED & WARD

Franklin, Wisconsin

As an apostolate of the Priests of the Sacred Heart, a Catholic religious congregation, the mission of Sheed & Ward is to publish books of contemporary impact and enduring merit in Catholic Christian thought and action. The books published, however, reflect the opinion of their authors and are not meant to represent the official position of the Priests of the Sacred Heart.

2001

Sheed & Ward
7373 South Lovers Lane Road
Franklin, Wisconsin 53132
1-800-266-5564

Portions of this book have previously appeared in *Chicken Soup for the Expectant Mother's Soul*; the *Chicago Tribune*; the Pioneer Press newspapers; the Crossroad Center's magazine, *The Works: Your Source for Being Fully Alive*; and the author's Internet column "Moments Online."

Printed in the United States of America

Cover design: Kathy Kikkert
Cover photography by Shouichi Itoga/Photonica
Interior design: GrafixStudio, Inc.
Author photo by DiNanno Photography, Inc., Northbrook, IL

Library of Congress Cataloging-in-Publication Data

Warda, Jim.
    Where are we going so fast? : finding the sacred in everyday
moments / Jim Warda; foreword by Jack Canfield.
        p. cm.
    ISBN 1-58051-096-5
        1. Spiritual life. I. Title
    BL624 .W343 2001 BV 4501. 2. W343
    291.4--dc21   2001
                                                            2001020135

1 2 3 4 5 / 04 03 02 01

dedication

For my dad,
who taught me everything I needed to know
about courage and truth.
He was a warrior.
He was a writer.
But, most of all, he was my hero.

contents

foreword

I first came across Jim Warda's writing when he contributed two remarkable stories to our *Chicken Soup for the Expectant Mother's Soul*. Intrigued by his ability to find sacred lessons in the ordinary moments, I began reading his weekly Internet column, "Moments Online."

Since that time, I've become a real fan of Jim's work and dedication to revealing his life. Most important, he offers his moments compassionately and allows us to watch through his eyes as he struggles with the human condition. Then, by watching him find and lose and find his way again, we come to understand so much more about our own search.

Whether it's as a compelling writer for the *Chicago Tribune*, delivering keynote speeches, presenting workshops, or recording his daily radio show, Jim is courageously committed to being authentic, as he is in this book. And, because of this commitment, we always come away from his stories knowing that we've heard something special and, most assuredly, real.

In fact, that is one of the main reasons I wanted to introduce *where are we going so fast? finding the sacred in everyday moments*. Another is that I believe in its message. Namely, that our moments contain sacred lessons and that sharing these moments connects us. Finally, there's the most obvious reason, which is simply that Jim's a very good writer.

In this wise, caring book, Jim repeatedly asks the question, "where are we going so fast?" and forces us to take a closer look at our lives and how we're living them.

So, after reading the book, I think you'll find yourself looking at your life and the world in a different way. And I think you'll be happier and more alive because you took the time to notice.

Finally, Jim's mission is very much like ours at Chicken Soup for the Soul Enterprises, which is "to change the world one story at a time." That must be why his stories touch me. And, that is exactly why you must read this book. Because, although it may seem that he's writing only about his life, he's really writing about you and me.

Enjoy, my friend!

—Jack Canfield
Co-author, the Chicken Soup for the Soul series

noticing
our
moments

~

We do not remember days,
we remember moments.
—Cesar Pavese

the answer came, as it does, in moments

I took my dad to the doctor, one of his many follow-up visits after bypass surgery. In the office, I helped him take off his coat, his sweater, and then his shirt. Layers of clothing on a warm October day because the surgery had taken something out of him.

Finally, I helped him take off his T-shirt, only to be struck silent by how thin he had become. In that cold, sterile room, with my dad's eyes numbed by fear of what the doctor might say, all I remember was the outline of his ribs and the scar cutting down his chest.

He'd been quiet since we left the house and I knew he was scared. After all, he'd been told that he may need further surgery. So, as he waited, I guessed that he was expecting the worst. But, instead, the doctor examined him and said, "Well, everything looks okay. Let's see you again in two months." Then, the doctor walked out, not noticing our relieved faces or the slow unclenching of my father's hands.

Later, we walked back to the car with the sun at our backs. As we did, our shadows played ahead on the sidewalk, slipping over the cracks to briefly join and then break apart.

At home that night, I started to help my son, Jeremy, take off his T-shirt for a bath. But just as I pulled the shirt over his head, something happened to my eyes. Like seeing the moon released from the clouds, I suddenly saw what I had not seen—a connection between the moment I'd shared that day with my father and that moment, there, with my son.

Trying to define that connection, I finally discovered it in the fact that I would probably be helping my dad take off his shirt for the rest of his life but, that soon, my son would be taking his shirt off by himself. A moment of sadness and wonder. Of waking to the realization that there might be a whole sacred world behind and within the world we see.

And it was right then, kneeling on the bathroom floor, that this book was born. An inglorious setting perhaps, but, looking back at it now, one that was certainly inevitable.

Because my life had been building to that moment. A life filled with struggling to find truth, courage, and everything else that keeps us in churches, synagogues, mosques, and other holy places that promise meaning. A life spent searching for a reason to believe.

And one spent learning to write. A profession that, because it demands observation and attention to branches and baby's eyes, prepared me to notice the moments.

So, having seen, the very next thing I wanted to do was share what I had found. Because I quickly realized that if I saw those connections in my moments, you could see them in yours. And that when you did, you would find similar truths.

When we share our moments, we become connected by the lessons they hold. Lessons that, when laid side by side, corner to corner, touch something greater and more powerful than each of us can know alone. Lessons that lead us to the most certain fact that we are loved and must, therefore, treat each other lovingly. And lessons that connect us to a force that just might be the tender hand of God.

this book of stones

This book is built of stones. Stones of words I began writing for the Pioneer Press newspapers and now for the *Chicago Tribune*. Words you'll find in The Crossroad Center's magazine, *The Works*. Words from my contributions to *Chicken Soup for the Expectant Mother's Soul*. And finally, words from my Internet column, "Moments

Online," through which thousands of readers have formed a community.

Many of the stories in this book are about my wife and children. I married Gina and her son, Jeremy (eight), five years ago. Since then, we have had Matthew (four) and, most recently, our baby daughter, Alexandra Marie (six months). They are the biggest part of this book because, without them, I would never have seen.

Because this book is organized around several themes, you will find that the stories do not appear in chronological order. So if Jeremy goes from seven years old to one year old in the blink of an eye, you'll understand. And if turning the page changes summer into winter with no autumn to cushion the blow, you'll know why.

You'll also read about the rest of my family, along with others who've taught me so much. And, through it all, you'll find you. Because, although the stories are mine, they are yours, too. Between the commas and the breaths between the words are the things we all share.

what's it all about?

This book is about the way we can wake to meaning in the ordinary moments. How we believe in something and doubt it all at the same time. How we desperately want to have courage although we're half-frozen in fear. How love and family are the flesh we build our lives upon. How we stumble upon the fact that in life there is death, and in death there is life, and that the line between the two often fades.

Most important, though, you'll read in this book the message that we're not alone, that we're loved, and that we're connected. A connection that honors us with a responsibility to one another.

Finally, at the end of each section, you'll find several questions that may help you find the lessons in your life.

why we share

A priest once told me why the Church often sent missionaries to spread the word in twos and not alone. After all, more people would hear their message if they went out individually. The priest said that missionaries went out in pairs so that they could share their experiences with each other. "Because," he went on to explain, "until you share your stories, they're not real. When you see a magnificent sunrise, the first thing you want to do is tell someone about it. Then it becomes real for you."

My gift to you is that I saw something that I want to tell you about. Your gift to me is that you're listening and want to share your stories with me. And for that, I can't thank you enough.

—Jim R. Warda
Gurnee, Illinois

where are
we going
so fast?

∼

No matter how slow the film,
Spirit always stands still long
enough for the photographer
It has chosen.
—Minor White,
Photographer

where are we going so fast?

I often hear people say things like, "I ran out the door so quickly this morning that I don't even remember if I kissed the kids" and "I know I should slow down, but I just can't find the time."

Where are we going so fast?

And, what can we do to find meaning in our moments?

Slowing down isn't the only answer. Just as important is noticing what's happening around and through us once we've put our burdens aside. Because none of this life we're living will mean very much if we don't pay attention to what's most important on this ride.

So, in this section, let's first talk about noticing the moments. And let's notice what we haven't noticed, the moments that escaped without a farewell party. Those moments that haunt us, the ones we'll probably regret not having spent more time living. Those moments that meant the most but mattered least when they happened because there was so much more to think about—like going to the mall or cleaning the garage.

Moments that left us searching for answers, although we didn't have enough words to form the questions. That left us looking for ways to fill the hole that opened up when we first believed that we weren't good enough and that there was no meaning except the ten o'clock news. That instilled in us a belief that we can't share our fear with the people out there because they fly by with their smiles and you're sure that they're sure that they're fine and they fit.

And then let's discuss the fact that we can't fill those holes with dollar bills or mend our hearts with new cars. That we're all confused at times, wondering who we are and why we're here, and hoping there's a Force to be with us as Obi-Wan promised.

So let's agree that there are lessons bound in the stories of glory and tears we live each day, waiting for us to look at them in just the right light or with just the right eyes.

And let's ask the real question: "Where are we going so fast?" Then, as we do, we realize that all the meaning we ever need is already here.

It's all here, just waiting to be found, wondering when we're ever going to take the time to realize that we are surrounded, even penetrated, by the sacred, soaked in its sacramental waters and held close to its loving lips.

It's all here, just waiting to connect us.

So let's begin this search together. And, if it gets dark and looks like rain, just take my hand. Because the road is longer, and so much harder, when you're alone.

where are we going
so fast?

I almost missed it. Almost walked straight through without once noticing where I was or what I was running to and from.

After all, it was only a blur, a flash of color and light that I almost mistook for taillights past the window.

Because, just like you, I was busy. Busy paying bills and collecting paychecks. Busy changing the oil in my car when it was really me who needed the tune-up.

Busy looking everywhere but inside, searching for meaning in "Self-help" aisles and the manic voices of motivational speakers. Not quite understanding that nothing outside of me could make up for the place in my heart where I was alone.

So, in the middle and midst of life, I stopped. Actually, someone stopped me. And, to be exact, it was two some-ones: my wife and my son. Because falling in love with them slapped me across my sleeping face and woke me to the fact that if I didn't start noticing what was going on around me, I was going to die never having tasted the moon.

So I hit the brakes, crunched to a halt, and looked left and right and left again, to check for oncoming cars and any sign of revelations.

And, in that stopping, in that moment, I found some-thing sacred, something solid and true. The moments that connect us and make us responsible to and for one another.

Moments in our lives, in the quietest corners of each day, that fold over each other like baby's arms. Ones that can slip by, into the throat of the night, if we're not awake.

So what about you? What about your moments? What would you say if I asked if you saw the sunrise today? Or kissed someone and left them knowing that you couldn't possibly love them more? Or decided, once and for all, that you were going to take the day off to tango?

After all, what could possibly be more important than our moments? Especially as so many of us move faster than the speed of enlightenment, choking down sandwiches and newspapers while we're intertwined in the Internet.

So, in this fad of madness, I share a moment that taught me the pain that most surely comes if we forget ourselves on this ride.

You see, yesterday, Matthew, my youngest son, woke up crying at 3:17 a.m. As he did, I made my way into his room, missing everything in front of me as I began thinking about the day ahead.

I walked over to his crib and picked him up. But I may have missed his first smile of the morning because I was thinking through my morning meetings.

Then I sat and held him as he put his head against my chest. But I may have missed him looking up at me while I was trying to find the remote to catch the news.

And that's when I realized that the only news that mattered was the child in my arms. For, in that moment, I'd been far away, missing my son and my life.

For, as I searched for the remote, Matthew reached his hand out and touched my lips. I was about to move it but then my eyes couldn't leave his fingers, couldn't deny the fact that I saw the future there . . .

. . . and that hand dipping in fingerpaints, scooping out pumpkins, throwing a baseball, hugging his mom, wiping awkward teenage tears, signing a driver's license then a marriage license, holding his sleeping baby daughter, and helping me out of a chair when I'm older.

I saw those gentle fingers become a boy's, then a man's. It happened quickly . . . and then was gone. Like a firefly.

I saw all of that at 3:17 a.m. But I could just as easily have missed it. Again, I ask, "Where are we going so fast?"

so hungry

I'm hungry, and, I can tell by your eyes that you're hungry, too.

Hungrier than we ever imagined we could be. But not for food. No, what we're hungry for can't be found in gro-cery-store aisles. And the dishes that come out of bright blue Italian kitchens couldn't begin to touch the place inside that aches.

Because our hunger is for connection. Connection with the faces that move past us each day. Connection that reveals that we do belong to something just as divine as what stares back at us while we brush our teeth and con-template our hair.

But in order to connect, I do believe that we must first reveal exactly who we are.

Because if we don't, we'll just stop on the street to talk about the weather without once touching on how much we miss each other.

Or we'll sit in meeting rooms and discuss projects without once asking why we aren't both doing what we love to do and, instead, are wasting the skin off our hearts.

I'm hungry. Hungrier than I ever imagined I could be. And that is why I'm writing these words and sending out these pleas.

So am I alone? I don't think so. After all, you're right there and I can tell by your eyes that you're hungry, too.

sacred planes

I want to show you something sacred.

It's just over there, past the roller coaster and the cotton candy. Yes, there it is—the children's airplane ride. You know the one. Red-and-white planes that go around and up and down.

Now just stand here a minute. It'll start soon. But once it does, you'll have to pay attention. Because sacred things can happen fast.

Okay, the planes are moving. Most of the children are smiling but there are a few younger ones close to tears. But luckily, flying can stop crying in a heartbeat.

Now watch closely. No, no, not the children. Watch the parents. Yes, the ones standing at the fence around the ride. Watch their faces. Watch them wave. Watch them yell their child's name. Watch them yell directions on how to work the stick.

And as you do, you'll notice the sacred thing shooting from their mouths and fingertips. It's love.

On parents' faces as they see their children through starry, starry eyes. On children's faces as they catch sight of their parents each time around. And for both, it's like the first time they ever laid eyes on each other.

So what do you think? Are you glad you came?

And, most important, where should we go next—the Ladybugs or the Train? I hear the Train's got some sacred tracks.

what makes it precious
is that it ends

What makes it precious is that it ends.

Tonight, near the end of a family party, our boys and my brother's girls had more than enough energy left to dance. And, luckily, we had our Backstreet Boys tape.

So we turned off the lights, started the music, and my father-in-law twirled flashlights to create a lightshow.

Jeremy moved left then quickly right, a Tony Monero for the new millennium. Madeline, my brother's oldest, and our son Matthew became Astaire and Rogers, floating just above the floor. While, Elise, their youngest, walked through it all, laughing.

Surrounding them were my parents and in-laws, my brother and his wife, my sister and her husband, and my wife with our new baby inside her, clapping, pointing, and caught in a moment that will never be again.

I took it in, as I always do. Photographed their laughter. Took notes in my heart and wanted it to remain. But, of course, it had to end. And it always ends. I know that.

But that doesn't mean I'm happy about it. In fact, it often hurts and threatens to ruin moments for me because I'm looking ahead to when they will be gone.

Although, lately, I'm learning, finding that it's the things we do today that matter most. And that it's the ending itself that makes it precious.

Actually, it's probably a good thing moments end.

Because endless moments might not mean as much.

twenty ways
to feed your soul

How do we feed our soul? I mean, we do so much for everything else in our lives. We eat to stay strong. We fill up the car to get from here to there and back again. And we make sure the smoke detector's got a new battery.

But what about our soul? How do we keep it fresh even on the days when the world's too busy to notice that we're out of breath?

Well, here are a few suggestions:

1. Think about Yoda more often.
2. Look at the pictures that people have in their homes, in their wallets, and on their desks. These pictures tapestry their lives.
3. If you know someone who lost someone sometime ago, ask them how they're doing. Grief doesn't always show up on a face or in small talk.
4. Listen to a child laugh. Just listen.
5. Find your purpose. Discover your special gift to the rest of us and begin to use it. We'd all appreciate it.
6. Read a book about something that has nothing to do with logic or the daily grind. You might start with *Callings: Finding and Following an Authentic Life* by Gregg Levoy.
7. Smile. It's amazing. People usually smile back.
8. Sing. Sing a song. Make it simple to last your whole life long.

9. At some point today, dance. If you happen to choose a time when you're at a store or waiting in the dentist's office, I'd suggest something from *Grease*.

10. Laugh loud enough to shatter each of Saturn's rings— twice.

11. Believe you can fly. Where would you go first? Who would you show off for?

12. As you're grocery shopping, start to skip. Then watch as everyone else in the store follows along.

13. Tell the people you love why you love them, and make darn sure they know that they're the reason you breathe.

14. Decide once and for all that you'll learn all the words to the Banana Splits' theme song.

15. Bring the passion from your heart to your hands.

16. Smell the rain, fresh-baked bread, and babies.

17. Know that we stand stronger together than apart.

18. Find Bruce Springsteen's "Born to Run" on the car radio, roll down the window, and let the wind make its way through his words.

19. Understand that you can do almost anything you set your mind to. The hardest part is setting your mind.

20. E-mail me at Wordwind5@aol.com and tell me some more ways to feed our souls.

how the grinch
saved christmas

The Grinch was the best thing that ever happened to the Whos.

I remember watching Dr. Seuss's "How the Grinch Stole Christmas!" as a kid. Most of all, I was amazed at how all the Whos down in Who-ville still celebrated Christmas even though they'd lost so much. And how they still gathered in the center of town to join hands and sing.

But along with my amazement came a fervent prayer that I'd never be put in that situation. Because I couldn't quite imagine Christmas morning without a tree to run to, presents to open, or the wait for my father to put together all the toys.

In fact, if someone had taken our family's presents and tree, I doubt very highly that my first reaction would have been to sing. No, more likely, I would have encouraged my dad to call the police and set up roadblocks.

And, for a child, that's okay. In fact, it's expected. Because, as much as we tell our children about Christmas being a season for love, keeping them focused on the birth of a child two thousand years ago when the local toy store's having a sale is the closest thing to impossible I know.

But, as we grow, things change. As they tend to do.

For me, in fact, they have changed so much that I now find myself understanding the Whos and the Grinch a little better. Because, by doing what he did, the Grinch offered the Whos the greatest gift, the chance to remember that "Christmas" is really just a longer word for "love."

A love found in the moments. The moments that ornament our life if we take the time to notice them. The moments found in days and nights having nothing to do with money orders, catalogs, or ATMs. In stories of caring and knowing that, without love, there really is very little reason to sing.

When I finally opened my eyes, I found that love on Christmas Eve, as my family gathered at my sister's house, warmed by the fire and the clear, perfect truth that we were together.

Love as my brother-in-law or nephew dressed up as Santa and went outside to ring jingle bells. Then, love as we watched the children run through the house, window to window, yelling, "He's here! He's here!"

Love in driving home later that night, most certainly a silent night since our children had fallen asleep, casualties of the holiday's chocolate feast, which even then streaked their faces.

Love, years later, as Gina and I sat with our boys next to the Christmas tree. The only lights on in the house were those on the tree, reflected in their eyes.

Love as we then told them the history of each ornament. Because, in our family, each ornament has a story. And every story has its telling.

Love in the moments with my father, hugging him awkwardly as his rough lips and stubble brushed against my cheek.

Love in the coming Christmas with our new baby daughter, Alexandra.

And, sadly now, love as we face our first Christmas without my dad, who died this year.

These moments tell me again that Christmas isn't about the biggest gift or the largest credit card balance. Instead, as the Grinch showed me as a child, there's nothing I can touch, taste, see, hold, or hear that will mean more than those sweet moments.

So, I'll remember the Grinch and his lessons. That on Christmas morning, new slippers and diamond earrings are no match for a child's smile or a father's kiss. And that, if we believe, our hearts, too, can grow three sizes, maybe more, just by noticing that what matters the most usually costs nothing at all.

All references and excerpts from *How the Grinch Stole Christmas!* by Dr. Seuss (Random House, 1957).

warning: this may cause you discomfort

Someone once said that my writing made them uncomfortable, with its searching and stirring in vulnerable places, like fear and love. Now when I first heard this, I was concerned. After all, how many writers do you know who want to bother their readers?

Well, now you know one.

Because that is exactly my intent. You see, I never wanted to be a "thought for the day," choking on clichés or serving up heaping plates of platitudes. There are enough of those to go around.

No, this is simply you and me making our way together, sharing stories and drinking as deep as we dare of sweetbitter truth.

I think we need to be uncomfortable, for it seems that it is only in those waters that we learn.

And, as you can probably tell, I'm uncomfortable. Have been. Probably always will be. Because there is something I am doing, saying, walking toward, hearing, singing, bathing in, running through, dancing upon. Something that burns me pure in its pursuit.

So why are you here? What great thing do you intend? And, if it is awesome and will make us better, when will you begin? Or have you already?

Uncomfortable. For me, there is no finer place to start.

a little wish

Yesterday, Jeremy, my seven-year-old, told me about a book he was reading. In it, a child releases a genie from a bottle and is granted a wish.

And that got me thinking. What would I wish for?

The first things that came to mind were the usual suspects like money and fame. But then, as I moved deeper into the question, I started thinking about the sacred things a wish could bring.

Like happiness for my family. Like walking into oncology wards and laying my hand upon sunken, weakened shoulders until faces grew pink and full and ready once again to laugh. Like making broken hearts whole or easing the suffering that can come in the middle of the night when we realize that our dreams have died.

And it also came to me that I couldn't make the wish alone. That we'd need to do it together. Because, as always, whatever one does, we all do.

So, my friend, what is your wish? What one thing matters most to you?

Don't worry. Take your time. Just make it count.

do not suffer liars

There are people on the edges of my life who lie like we breathe, their words soaked in oil. I try to climb their proclamations but find no purchase. With fingers reaching for a hold, I search for the truth. But, instead, the liar lies again and the ledge disappears beneath me. Then I fall, simply saying, "I never knew there was such evil."

These liars tell me something each time they lie. They tell me that they don't care. They tell me that they'd rather hide who and what they are than be exposed.

But, as always, it begins with trust. When trust is strong, there's nothing finer. I can turn to tomorrow with you at my back, and still be safe. You won't harm me. I trust.

But when people lie, they rip the stones out from under our feet. And things will never be the same.

So, then, how to fight liars? Do we duel with the same weapon and call for "lies at dawn"? Or do we brandish truth?

Yes, truth is the answer. Hold to it—even when the ledge is gone. For nothing is more beautiful than those who fight the dark.

I do not suffer liars well. But I believe that liars do, indeed, suffer.

was there something?

Was there something you wanted to do with your life, something that slipped through the cracks between your days?

Was there someone you loved who never knew?

Are you doing exactly what you were put here to do?

And where are you going so fast?

Then, what would you die for?

Then, who would you live for?

And, if you are hiding, what would happen if, for one perfect moment, you took off your faces and let us see exactly who you are?

Are you afraid that we wouldn't love you?

Or, worse, are you afraid that we would?

do you believe in magic?

Children see with pure hearts, undaunted by skeptics or pessimists.

Every day I try to see that way, too. To believe in the power of things that can't be touched. But, as an adult, I struggle to quiet a churning brain and instead listen to their innocent whispers.

Last week, in a shopping mall, I heard those whispers while standing at the wishing fountain with my son, Matthew. He was looking up eagerly at Gina, waiting for pennies. But, since she had only one, I told him to make sure he made a good wish.

With that, he closed his eyes, moved his lips silently to form the words, and then snapped his arm forward. The penny shot through the air and slammed into the fountain's steps. It then tumbled until it came to rest on the lowest ledge, well within my reach.

And, at that moment, my brain spoke to me. My brain, the adult *me* that only believes what is seen, only knows what is known, and cannot imagine that magic has its place.

It told me to remove the coin that Matthew had thrown and give it back to him so he could try again. "After all," it explained, "what difference will it make if he throws it again?"

Unable to disagree, I reached for the coin. But, just then, my heart interrupted, that *me* more ready to admit that there just might be some mystery to this earth.

"Wait a second, Bucko!" my heart yelled.

"What's wrong?" I asked, not liking to be called "Bucko" by an internal organ.

"Now, Jim," my heart began, in a lecturing tone. "You know it's not right to take a coin out of a fountain. Don't you remember that day several years ago when you and Jeremy (my other son) threw coins in the pool at the amusement park?"

"Yes, so?"

"Well, do you remember what Jeremy asked you after he made his wish?" my heart asked.

"Yeah. He wanted to know what would happen to the coins."

"What'd you tell him?" my heart continued, in a most uncomfortable line of questioning.

"I told him that workers probably removed the coins each night and donated them to charity."

"And what did he say to that?" my heart asked, growing impatient.

"He was worried about what would happen to the wishes of all the kids who'd thrown in their coins. He said their wishes wouldn't come true if their coins were taken out."

And right then I realized what my heart was getting at. You see, Jeremy asked that question because he believes in the power of wishing on a coin. But, because I'm an adult and usually believe only in what I see, I don't believe in wishes.

And that's terribly sad. Because when we lose that sacred part of ourselves, life's sweet mystery has a way of fading into errands and bills, with the only uncertainty being when we're going to schedule our next dentist appointment.

"Well?" my heart interrupted, waiting.

"Well, what?"

"Well, what are you going to do?" it asked.

As my answer, I slowly pulled my hand back and gave up the idea of taking back the penny. After all, how did I know that taking the coin out wouldn't affect Matthew's wish? Because, after thinking about it, I realized that I've seen too many things on this little green planet not to believe in magic.

I've seen people suffer yet somehow find the strength to carry on. I've seen broken-hearted men and women crash back into the belly of love. I've seen the sunrise give dreamers back their dreams. And, I've seen my children born, and stood amazed as my heart grew to accommodate that new love.

No, I wouldn't remove the coin. Instead, I'd make a wish myself, that Matthew's wish would come true.

questions

what moments have changed your life?

what moments would you most like to live again, that you may have missed the first time around?

what was the best day of your life?

what one thing will you do today to notice your moments?

how will you teach the children to notice their moments?

part two

in the dance
of faith
and fear

∽

*The courage of very ordinary
people is all that stands
between us and the dark.*
—Pam Brown

in the dance of faith and fear, it all comes down to the
same defining moment: will you believe?

Will you believe when every sunrise finds you contemplating another day of trying to get it right? Will your
faith stay strong in the hospital halls, walking past kids
with cancer who won't live long enough to dance at their
prom? Will you have courage when you need to say "No"
to someone who only hears "Yes"?

Difficult questions. But gifts also. Because if we
attempt to answer them, they help us find ourselves. For,
keeping the faith when even the trees haunt us, or walking

into fear when even our tendons tighten seems to be the surest way back to who we are.

And who we are comes in the decisions, when we either begin to move, believing that the path will appear under our feet as we go, or swear off paths forever. The days when what we most want to do is curl up in the comfortable instead of tasting something new. The nights when the very last thing we want to feel is the damp chill against our skin as we make our way.

These are the moments, the sacred chances for us to become something else, something more divine.

Now, for me—and maybe for you—it's always a struggle, and I keep waiting for the day when I'll be able to believe easy, without a cloud of doubt. But it never happens. I always have doubts. And often, there's fear.

But, I've come to believe that doubt and fear are essential to this human condition, the price and the blessing of being us, the sound of the sacred being shaken and stirred. Because courage only comes when we're afraid. And faith grows when we believe in the face of doubt.

So maybe we need to not only accept but also embrace this doubt and fear. For, in that embrace, there may be the whispers of salvation, a promise from the mouth of God that we are worthy, that we belong, and that we are most truly loved.

If that's the case, then, we may want to hold our doubts and fears a little closer. Sweep aside the dirt and the dust until we come to their centers. And then, once we do, stand amazed at the fact that what really exists there is our faith and our courage. Allies who have simply been biding their time until, like Dorothy in Oz, we believed in ourselves.

So, today, let's move, take action, and shout, "We're alive, we doubt, and, by golly, we're afraid!" Words that will free us, will remove the shame that we've felt for so long about not feeling perfect and divine and ready to stand trial.

And, in this section, let's expect to struggle. In fact, let's look forward to it. Because my struggle, so very much like yours, is to be strong in the face of doubt and fear. To cling to the mountain when all that's below is a long, slow drop into despair. To believe in a God who also made cancer. To figure out what we believe in, what we would fight for, and even what we would die for, if dying was the only way.

So, we'll share this dance with faith and fear. With our faces pressed against their shoulders, saying how badly we want to believe. Fear just mocks us but faith brushes the hair off our foreheads and whispers that everything's going to be okay, that even the strongest of us falters, and that no matter what, the dance will always end with a kiss.

i believe

- I believe.

- I believe in love because my wife taught me how.

- I believe that a dance with fear leaves you winded, yet wiser.

- I believe that having children has made me a better man.

- I believe Speed Racer knew that Racer X was really his brother.

- I believe that truth tastes like strawberries—the really big ones.

- I believe in friends who stand by you.

- I believe you have to suffer for your passion.

- I believe that the happiest people are those with the fewest masks.

- I believe that too many people stay at jobs they hate to get more vacation days so that they can spend more time away from the jobs they hate.

- I believe that we give life its meaning.

- I believe that John really did believe in what he did with The Beatles.

- I believe that liars run from the truth like vampires from the sun.

- I believe that the Force is always with us.

- I believe that Rudolph never really got over the fact that the other reindeers wouldn't let him play in their games.

- I believe that courage works its way from the heart to the hands.

- I believe that knowing yourself is one of the finest things you can do.

- I believe in blue kites with orange tails.

- I believe in living passionately, leaving nothing inside, bringing it hard and fast like a steam train, and touching souls.

- I believe in making yourself vulnerable to find your strength.

- I believe in listening for the sound of your own voice.

- I believe in you.

What do you believe in?

you're going to change the world

You're going to change the world today.

No, don't try to deny it. And you know, I understand that it can be a little overwhelming, to have the entire world depending on you. But I know that you can do it.

Actually, I knew you could do it when I first met you. When I first saw the hunger in your fingertips and the fire in your eyes.

When you spoke in just that way, with just those words, in just that rhythm that said, "I'm going to change the world. Gonna make it a little better, a little sweeter, a bit more true."

And I remember the way you said that nothing on this or any other planet was going to stop you. Then you turned and walked away, confident and clear.

And I remember thinking to myself that you were amazing, that I'd never met anyone quite like you, and I was sure that, if you put your mind and hands to it, there was nothing that could break you.

So there you sit, knowing that today's the day. Because I see the way you're shifting nervously in your chair, the way your body crackles and zaps, the way your grin says that you've decided that there is no time like now to move.

You're going to change the world today. I'm just glad I was here to see it.

are you afraid?

Is there something that you're careful to walk around so that you won't be caught by its loving arms?

And if you are afraid, would you tell me?

Would you say, "Jim, I don't want to fall in love again because it scares me"? Or would you whisper about the dream you buried on a November night behind the house, the dream you killed by moonlight because you were so terrified of being told you weren't good enough?

Now, wait. You see, I promise to be gentle with your fear just as you are with mine.

After all, if we can't share what makes us human, then what are we doing here? If I can't tell you that, sometimes, I get so frightened in the places where the valves of my heart cast their richest shadows, then what good am I as a writer or, even more, as a friend?

And then you ask, "How can we be friends?" when all I do is write for you, for me.

But you must know that it's my flesh you're reading here and that it's your listening and sharing that matters.

So if you're afraid and if I'm afraid, then the best we can do is walk into the darkest part of the forest together. And, when we do, let's stay close and committed. After all, that's what forests are for.

the truth and
clipping nails

Clipping Matthew's nails was a moment of truth.

My two-year-old sat on our bed, fidgeting and close to tears. You see, he didn't like having his nails trimmed. But still, I prepared, positioning the lamp surgeon-like, carefully checking my instruments. Then I turned to my most important preparation—easing his mind.

Knowing how worried he was, I began to rub his back and reassure him, saying, "It'll be all right. Daddy's here." With that, he relaxed a bit and offered his hand. So I began.

First, the thumb. Then, the pointer. As I worked, Matthew bit his lip, obviously worried. But I was already in the zone, moving left then right in furious concentration.

After several minutes, I moved on, until time itself seemed to disappear. Finally, I reached my ultimate challenge, my Everest—the pinky. I clipped faster yet with greater precision. My movements blurred as the clipped nails plinked against the inside of the garbage can and the clipper danced closer to his skin. Until, finally, I was done.

Which is when I noticed Matthew smiling up at me, as if he had just figured out that, with his dad around, he'd be safe.

And I realized again that I was no longer just a man pretending to be a dad, trying to hide the fact that he didn't have anything on his resume even remotely resembling the qualifications needed for the job.

No, my son trusted me. What else is there?

saving captain warda

And if I didn't return?
What matter; At least this much
We were the whirlwind,
promised by the above,
and He said there is no greater love
than to heroically save others.
So, with this resolved,
we took off into the fray.
—Robert Warda

My Dad gave names to the dead men. Only the ones he knew, though. And, as he spoke, their ghosts came off him like steam.

During World War II, my dad was a captain and navigator in B-26 Marauder bombers with the Ninth Air Force, first in England, then in France. Like many veterans, he rarely spoke about what he'd seen and done during the war. But I knew it lived in him, bullied its way through his blood, and swore it would never let him forget.

I'm not sure, though, that I realized just how much he had suffered. Because, like most, I've never known battle. However, as years passed, we talked more about his experiences.

As we did, his stories came. Slow and heavy because they hadn't been shared before. So many moments that boy-man in his twenties might have died. When the anti-aircraft guns found his plane and sent hot metal through his leg. Or when his other plane, "Nick's Chick," was shredded by flak and crashed. And the mission where his pilot asked if my dad could lead over sixty bombers out of occupied France. He was lost but didn't let on. Instead, he found a way.

My dad also told me how, before each mission, he'd ask himself, "Why am I here? What am I fighting for?"

His answer came on a bitter winter's morning in Pontoise, France. As his squadron prepared to take off, he saw barefoot children being led to school through the freezing snow, the war having left them with little food or clothes. And that sight gave him his reason—to protect the children.

So, as I listened to the stories, I realized that my father needed to heal, to let go. Although he'd never say it, he wanted to know someone saw what he and the others did, and understood.

Someone finally said those words.

It happened when a U.S. army commander led a ceremony in which she awarded my father the French Jubilee of Liberty Medal, which honored those who took part in D-Day.

She began by reading his story of that day. As she did, my father's eyes grew distant, and I knew he was reliving those horrible moments. Afterwards, declarations from France and the United States were read, thanking him for his service.

When those words were spoken, my father began to cry. I wanted to throw an arm around him, but I knew he was hearing what he most needed to hear. That his sacrifice and the sacrifice of all those who had fought and died had been remembered. And finally, after fifty-five years, he had been given a chance to grieve the good friends taken from him.

Later that night, I asked my dad what he would most like to say to those who honored him. His reply, "Thank you. Receiving that medal helped me realize that the war did happen, that it wasn't a dream, and that we really did save people."

You know, I do believe they saved Captain Warda.

what are you going to do?

Do you believe?

No, really, do you?

Do you believe in the truth that sits in each fold of your heart?

Do you believe in doing something that terrifies you just because it's right?

Do you believe in telling someone that you love them even if you can't see in their eyes whether or not they love you, too?

Do you believe that you could change the world for the better in a matter of minutes if you just put your mind, and hands, to it?

Do you believe in jumping through puddles rather than walking around?

Do you believe in never using the "snooze" button again and, instead, finding a job you love?

Do you believe in me?

Do you believe in you?

Then, if you believe, I have only one more question for you.

What are you going to do about it?

so many questions

I thought about giving up.

For a while, I didn't write. We moved to a new neighborhood five miles away from our old home that may as well have been five hundred, because it brought up the same old sadness I've always felt with good-byes.

And in a year filled with good-byes, it hurt to face another.

So, one night, when I should have been unpacking my computer, I decided not to. I told myself it was late and that I could write the next day.

But the next day came, and then another, and still my keyboard was silent.

Then, a friend asked why I hadn't written. I told him that I hadn't yet set up the computer. But, as soon as I said it, I realized that I was lying.

You see, the reason I wasn't writing was because I was angry and tired and I wanted to give up. Because trying to become a writer while deep in the middle of a full-time job is a life filled with rejection and people not calling you back when they said they would—and still my dad is gone.

And I wondered if anyone would notice if I stopped.

But today, in fact, right now, I've decided that giving up is not an option and never will be. Because this isn't about me. It never was. It's about us. And because these aren't my words. I'm only their caretaker.

And I have to write, to tell you about moments like last night when my son Jeremy hugged me hard as I pointed out the Big Dipper to him and then we played football under our new streetlight.

So I write. Not because I have the answers. But because there are still so many questions.

fighting our demons

I walk into my fear. But my son would rather take a roller coaster.

Last year, when we'd visit the amusement park near our house, Jeremy would refuse to go on the upside-down roller coasters. But, lately, something's changed.

In fact, yesterday, he decided to take on the Demon, one of the coasters that had always scared him.

Standing in line, I patiently answered each of his questions. Then, with a worried face, he told me that his stomach hurt and he wasn't sure if he wanted to ride.

So I put my arm around his shoulders and told him that he didn't have to, that we could get out of line and go on something easier. But, after thinking about it, he decided to try.

And it was then that I learned another lesson. Because watching your child walk into his fear can quickly make you commit to walking through your own.

So, after we boarded, I checked his harness and tried to distract him, hoping I could ease his mind. But that's where the second lesson came. Because I couldn't. No, he had to face his own demons. All I could do was be there.

Soon, after a quick drop, upside-down loops, and two corkscrews, we came back into the station. As we did, I looked over, expecting to see his eyes wide in fright or filled with tears. But, instead, he was smiling. Then he laughed and asked if we could ride again.

I walk into my fears. Jeremy takes a roller coaster. I think his way is a lot more fun.

voices

I hear voices.

When deep in the forest, my feet make no sound on this bed of wet leaves. As you know, I've been sent inside to face the darkest part of me. And I was sent alone.

Moving silent, the moon skips between branches and the grass is fog-hushed. But, now, I hear voices.

They urge me on, force me forward, when all I want to do is turn and run. In Camelot, the knights began their quest by entering the darkest part of the forest. Now I know why.

Because there is fear here. Cruel, like stone. It laughs at my weakness. Yet, I don't turn. I don't run. I move on, into its throat. Because of the voices.

You are the voices. You are my courage. Without you, I'd simply be one. Yet, with you, I am thousands. We are quiet on this journey. Words would waste. Instead, we share hearts.

So now, you take my hand and I yours. The forest is stranger here, stronger, more ready to bite. It crawls like a soldier, belly muddied, and eyes wide open. Smells like death. It wants you to forsake me and needs me to turn away.

Yet, I won't. And you don't. And with that decided, we move on, into the fear. Because, on the other side, we'll both be free.

i don't believe

- I don't believe in insincerity.

- I don't believe in lies.

- I don't believe in always being cautious.

- I don't believe in fear. Of course, I still fear. I just don't believe in it.

- I don't believe in letting love walk away if it's still bright blue and beating.

- I don't believe in going it alone.

- I don't believe in superficial conversations about the weather if I care about you. I'd rather know exactly who you are and what's sitting on the slightly pointed tip of your tongue.

- I don't believe in taking for granted.

- I don't believe in the terrible ways that we sometimes treat each other.

- I don't believe that Tennessee Tuxedo ever did fail.

- I don't believe in giving up the fight, no matter the cost.

- I don't believe in colorizing black-and-white movies, especially *It's a Wonderful Life*.

- I don't believe in UFOs, although I do believe some people are out of this world.

- I don't believe in evil. I mean, I know it exists. I just don't believe in it.

- I don't believe in painting pumpkins. I still feel that you need to get your hands in the goop and carve.

- I don't believe that the smallest piggy ever said, "'Wee, wee, wee' all the way home." Instead, I think he hung his head and walked dejectedly back to the barn, aware that he was, indeed, the end of the song.

- I don't believe in letting our older people leave this world without making sure we know exactly who they are, what they feel, and what they've learned.

What don't you believe in?

q u e s t i o n s

what is the most courageous thing you've ever done? how did you do it?

barring the death and sickness of you or a loved one, what are you most afraid of? how will you conquer that fear?

do you believe in God? all the time?

what three things do you most believe in? who do you most believe in?

how do you feel when you go strictly on faith?

and
do you
love?

~

Someday, after we have
mastered the winds,
the waves, the tides
and gravity,
we shall harness . . .
the energies of love.
Then, for the second time in
the history of the world,
man will have discovered fire.
—Pierre Teilhard de Chardin

and do you love?

Let's talk of love's voices. Of the ones we hear when the moon is high and crazy with dreams. Of the ones we speak when there's nothing left to say but "You do, indeed, amaze me."

And do you love the tender trails of kisses upon your hand? Or sitting at the bedside of a sick child, when the fever won't break but your heart's already begun? Or taking your mother's face in your hands to tell him that you're proud of the way he never gave up?

And do you love?

If you do, what responsibility do you have, a commitment that doesn't end just because things get difficult and so much more complicated?

Will we see it in your walk and the way you move? Will we know it by your eyes and the way you understand our weaknesses? Will we hear it in your words and the things you say about the way we leave you with a sense of wonder? And will we taste it through the times you help someone find their dignity again?

And do you love?

This, then, is love, that makes the world go 'round and our fragile hearts pound. But, alas, it comes to pass that love also has its price.

Because as soon as we love, we become vulnerable.

And in there, in the middle of that last sentence, is the most crucial question. Namely, will you love even though it means eventually losing who or what you love?

Will you believe in God although there's no real proof except the children and the trees? Will you die on a cross just to show the power of forgiveness?

Because love is a decision. One in which we choose to open ourselves, to put someone or something before us. And that, my friend, is where we become divine, where the universe plays alchemist and turns us slowly into gold.

After all, what else would make a man die on a cross or on the beaches of Normandy? And what else gives a

woman the strength to bring life into this world and protect it, although the way can be long and crammed with
heartache?

And do you love?

Love is the reason we were put here. For, in loving
and being loved, we become sacred. In giving of ourselves,
in moving past the fear of being hurt or letting go, we join
hands with every good thing on this planet.

In moving past the boundaries of our flesh to touch
another's heart, although we may not even know their
name or story. To crawl inside their lives with nothing but
a flashlight and the desire to let them know they're not
alone.

And do you love?

I was forced once again to answer this question after
my dad died, when my mom and I stood at his grave as she
asked me through tears, "Why does God put us on this
earth and then take us away?"

After a minute of silence, as I searched through my
files of faith and science, the only answer I could offer her
were three small words in the form of a question.

"Do you love?"

Because, if you do, Mom, and if you did, Dad, then
nothing else matters.

love in the
rearview mirror

I found love in the rearview mirror.

Over the weekend, my wife, the boys, and I were running errands in the minivan. But neither Jeremy nor Matthew had slept well the night before, so they were exhausted.

During the ride, Matthew's head started to bob as he fought to keep his eyes open. Soon, though, he fell asleep and his head dropped to the left, next to Jeremy.

At the same time, Jeremy, who was almost asleep himself, saw his brother's head dropping and moved to the right to support it with his shoulder. And, in a moment that will never leave me, he turned and gently kissed the top of Matthew's head, not knowing I was watching.

And that's where I began to worry. Because I knew that no matter how hard I tried, no matter what I wrote, I would never be able to capture that sacred moment when my sons became something else, something deeper than what we know.

Something that sits quietly behind what we see and taste, waiting patiently for us to discover it. Something that can be found in awkward first kisses, mothers rocking newborn babies, husbands whispering their wives' names, and the quiet moments of courage and caring that happen all around us.

But no matter how much I worry, I can't stop searching for the words. Because love wouldn't have it any other way.

valentine's

My wife's been gone for the weekend, and it's the best Valentine's gift I've ever received.

You see, lately, Gina and I have been caught up cold by the hurry and worry of life. She's taking care of the boys, running the house and, hardest of all, dealing with me. While I'm working, writing, doing workshops, and desperately trying to do home improvement projects without leaving cracks in the wall and scars on my arms.

Sadly, then, in the smack dab middle of this, it's easy to lose each other. To take each other for granted so much that the only time you talk is to say, "Have a good day" and "Sleep well, Honey."

So that's why my wife going to Las Vegas with her mom meant so much. Because it's given me a chance to remember exactly why I love her and what it was about her smile and the way she moved that captured me in the first place.

And, on this Valentine's Day, I've learned that having the chance to see what your life would be like without its blessings may be the greatest gift of all.

So, scattered amongst Valentine roses, you too can find Zuzu's petals.*

---

* From *It's a Wonderful Life*, starring Jimmy Stewart and Donna Reed (directed by Frank Capra, 1946).

have you tasted the moon?

In the middle of a July night, surrounded by your children, you look over at your husband. As you do, you think back to that first kiss with him. And you remember . . .

On a sweet, summer night, you're standing on the beach. He's next to you, with an arm around your waist.

Your mom told you that he wasn't any good for you. Your dad asked about his job. You answered, "He's a musician. He writes songs that make you wish you were the notes." Afterwards, your dad just grumbled and walked away.

Your mom turned to your dad later that night and gave him the "I can't believe we have to go through this again with her" look. Your dad shrugged his shoulders as if to say, "I know, but she is our daughter so we'll just have to make it through another weird boyfriend phase."

They didn't understand, couldn't comprehend, what it was like to stand on the sand with the world in his eyes. And just when you thought you could be here forever, watching the stars, he turns to you.

"Have you ever tasted the moon?" he asks.

"What?" you reply, caught in your thoughts and not quite sure if you'd heard him right.

"I said . . . have you ever tasted the moon?" he repeats, with a slight smile and his eyes staring into yours.

"Oh, come on," you laugh. "You can't do that!"

"Sure you can . . . if you want it bad enough," he explains. "Here, I'll show you. First, close your eyes."

So you do. Don't even ask why. Because you trust him. Actually, you love him. You haven't told him yet, but you're sure he knows.

As you close your eyes, he whispers, "Now, fly . . . lift your arms and let them be wings. Your feet rise from the sand. The night is chill but your heart burns. Tonight, you *will* taste the moon. And nothing *will* deny you.

"You begin to move, rising further. On and up, past meteors, through stars. Faster still. Soon, the moon bows before you and you bend to bite. Your head turns slightly, your mouth opens, and then . . . a crack of moon is clenched between your teeth. It breaks like waves and it's cold. You've tasted the moon and you swear it tastes like strawberries."

His words trail off and you stand there, in his spell. Slowly, you open your eyes and notice that he's still staring at you.

"Have I ever told you how beautiful you are?" he asks.

"Um, no, well . . . yeah, I guess you have," you reply, trembling.

"And have I ever told you how much I love you?" he asks.

"No . . . no, you haven't," you whisper.

"Well, you are and I do," he says, and kisses you.

And, as he does, you swear you taste the moon.

you are loved

How does that feel? Don't know? Okay, then let's try it again.

You are loved.

Still feel awkward? Do the words go straight to the saddest part of you, the part that someone said wasn't good enough? Well, if they do, I understand.

You see, I know what it's like to be scared that someone's going to see through me, going to look past the layers of skin and realize that I'm just some guy with a keyboard and a few words to spare.

But then, I reconsider and realize that I've got something to say.

So, again, I say it. "You are loved."

Now, understand, I love my wife. I love my boys and my girl. I love my family and friends, but when I say that "You are loved," it's not me who's doing the loving, though I'm sure I'd have great affection for you if we met.

So, if it's not me doing the loving, then who is it?

Well, that's up to you. Although I have a feeling that it has quite a bit to do with God and the way you're precious and understood. But, as I said, that's up to you.

The only thing that's not up to you is that you are loved.

m o m e n t s

Moments. These gifts in my life. I remember them all, the blessings that created the man who sits here typing, desperately wanting to make sense of this world. Thinking back . . .

To meeting Gina. Opened my door and there she stood. Hadn't seen her in a year, this woman who was my friend who became my wife. Her beauty hit me hard. I fell in love.

Then I met her son. Jeremy stumbled into my heart when he was one year old. I was playing guitar, something from the 70s, I think. Maybe "Billy, Don't Be a Hero." Then he touched the strings and I fell in love again.

Next, engagement in the city. I held out my hand to Gina. She stared at the horse-drawn carriage, amazed at the roses inside. Like a child, she took my hand as I helped her in.

As summer rained, I got down on a knee and spoke a line from my song, "Later that evening, in a carriage, a hundred white roses whispered marriage, would you be my wife?" She said, "Yes," and the world stopped—for just a moment.

A year gone by, to our wedding day. Peace. It flew by in a sparrow's breath. As the organ played "The Wedding March," I looked down the aisle into our future. Gina, a white flame. Holding her hand was Jeremy. And I thought about the precious gift that came to me.

Later, I placed a ring on her hand and said sacred things. After, I knelt to place a ring on her son's hand—

my son. I told him I'd always protect and love him. He smiled and I kissed his cheek. Then we lit a candle. In a moment, three became one.

Another moment. Matthew was busy being born. The doctor smiled and the room blurred. Nurses draped Gina's legs as I held the monitor on her stomach. Matthew's heart beat like hooves. And then he was there. The doctor handed him to us and we cried. So tiny. So perfect. This gift.

Moments join to make a life. These are mine. What are yours?

women, men,
and little rose soaps

I knew I was in trouble when my wife suggested redecorating.

With my mumbled "okay," we were off to the store, where we headed straight to the "Bath and Bedroom" section.

Gina walked wide-eyed through the bathroom accessories. They called to her, begging to be bought. To our left, a tapestry of towels sang of freshness and easy laundering.

I was simply bored. Because, as a man, I couldn't understand the attraction. Now, take me to a hardware store and I'll stand entranced by the dance of drills and hedgers. But soap dishes and toothbrush holders leave me unmoved.

As Gina made her way through the aisles, though, something came to me. The items on the shelves forced me to realize that Gina had taken over complete control of our house! I still commanded the garage, of course, but as far as everything else, I was as good as gone. It had been subtle, but swift.

For instance, the powder room. In that room, where very little powdering happens, there are many examples of how I, as a man, had lost control:

Little rose soaps. Soaps shaped like rosebuds that no one uses. In desperate times, when they're the only soap available, I've tried to use them. But I could only watch helplessly as they squirted out between my fingers and bounced against the bathroom—er, powder room—wall.

Guest towels. We spend our hard-earned money on towels and only guests can use them? Where, exactly, is the sense in that? How about if we use the nice ones and let them use our everyday ones? That sounds a little more equitable.

The knickknack shelf. As you'd guess, it's a small shelf on which you put knickknacks, like crystal clowns and dried-out flowers. "What are knickknacks?" some men might ask. As far as I can tell, they're items you put on shelves for one purpose only: so that when guests come over, they'll exclaim, "Oh my, you have the loveliest knick-knacks we've ever seen!"

The fake magazine collection. Magazines you never read that you put in your "powder room" solely to impress guests. For example, in ours, you'll find *Neurosurgeon Today* and *Gourmet Dining for Foreign Dignitaries.*

After the "Bathroom" aisle, I was reeling. But something far worse waited for me down the "Bedroom" aisle.

Pillow shams. Pillowcases for pillows that you never use. Their only purpose is to sit on the bed behind your real pillows to make the pillows you actually use look better.

The bed skirt. My wife said this was a decorative accent. For me, it's the sheet with ruffles that hides whatever you stick under your bed.

So, with our cart full of colors, fabrics, textures, and smells, we headed to the register. Gina had efficiently assembled a new powder room and bedroom while I was trying to make sense of the differences between men and women.

But as I did, I also realized that, aside from the obvious, we're quite similar. Because, even though I'd never use the rose-shaped soaps, there's something comforting about knowing they're there. And, although I can't even approach our guest towels without a deep sense of guilt, I do feel like royalty when we visit someone else and use theirs.

Crazy? Well, yes. But then again, who ever said the whole woman/man thing made sense. If it did, it probably wouldn't be half the fun.

a series of good-byes

September leaves arch this road, testament to another year that's passed into another year.

And, once again, I understand that life is a series of good-byes. Because people come and go. In fact, it seems like we're always saying good-bye to someone.

Some people enter and leave our lives in a heartbeat. They gently touch our hearts and are gone. But others weave themselves into who we are and what we believe.

As for me, I don't do well with good-byes. In fact, I'd much rather keep many of the people I've cared about around me forever. Of course, then we'd probably have to put on an addition.

Instead, when I look at good-bye as a way to live what I've learned from that person, I begin to see possibilities.

So I take at least one special thing about that person and bring it into my life. For instance, if that person stands up for what they believe in, I'll try harder to stand in the fire. If they laugh often, I'll try not to take life so seriously. By doing these simple things, then, I keep that person around even though they've gone, which is my way of honoring them.

Even those I consider not to be good people touch my life. I look at the evil or wrong they do and try to erase those things from my life, or at least reduce their power. If they've knocked a person down, I'll help that person stand. It doesn't always work. But I try.

So, if you have to say good-bye to someone today, take a moment to truly see them. Find something about them that moves you, and burn it into your brain. Then, swear that you will always carry them with you, wherever you go and however you are.

After all, we are who we've loved.

and she doesn't
even know

And she doesn't even know I'm watching

I wake up in the night, just enough to know I'm not dreaming. Looking to the left, I see Gina silhouetted against the nightlight. She's holding Alexandra and, from where I am, it seems like they're one. They are.

And she doesn't even know I'm watching.

I stand at my sister's house. Over my shoulder, I see her playing with my son, Matthew, helping him make holiday cards for the family. He colors quickly before putting them in an envelope they decorated together. My sister is patient and loving. My son is happy.

And she doesn't even know I'm watching.

My mother stands over my dad's grave, with her head bowed. She placed a porcelain angel near his headstone, "to protect him," she says. And, as she walks away with my arm around her, I know she struggles with the fact that he was here and now he's gone. She loves him so.

And she doesn't even know I'm watching.

In September, when I called my mother-in-law in the too-early morning to tell her Gina was having contractions, she told me she'd meet me at the hospital to pick up the boys. No hesitation, not a breath lost. She's always there when we need her. And we need her a lot.

And she doesn't even know I'm watching.

Alexandra and I watched football today. I held her in my arms as the Jets beat the Dolphins. I couldn't have cared less about the game. I just love to hold her.

And they don't even know I'm watching.

But I am.

steak through the heart

Something different in her eyes that night . . .

"I've met someone else," she said. And the whole world stopped, like a fossil.

You thought back to the last few months and it began to make sense. Clearer, like a river after the storm, after the mud's settled.

But your steak arrived just then. Looking down, you saw it sitting there, uncaring, unmoved by your predicament. Didn't she know that you never break up with someone while they're waiting for their steak?

And, at that precise moment, it began to hurt.

"Someone else," she had said. "Someone else," like it was just another day. Two words shouldn't dare to have so much power. And if they did, those words should have had to wait in line, tapping their feet nervously, before filling out a four-page application and going through a long interview process. That all should have happened before those two words hoped to have such strength.

But, as you looked back, you realized that those last months, she'd been acting differently. She didn't laugh at your jokes as much. Found reasons not to hold your hand. Passionate kisses turned to casual touches. And where she'd once adored you, there was mostly silence.

"Well, I hope you'll both be happy," you replied, not sure why. You just knew that that's what they say in the movies. And this felt like one of those old movies, where Humphrey Bogart tells someone something quick and cool.

She walked out then, crying. Because she remembered, too, that she'd once adored you. And you wondered how you got there from that first "Hello" at the graduation party where everyone faded away when you saw her.

You might have worked late one too many times or missed hearing something she'd said that was something she cared about that was something that mattered. Of course, it didn't matter anymore. She was gone.

Then months flew by. And now, a year later, you sit alone, holding your heart like a broken toy. Meanwhile, spring springs outside your window, along with swing-set chains and children's laughter at the park. But still you sit.

But soon, after handfuls of months, you'll meet someone new. She'll laugh and you'll smile. She'll breathe and you'll fill up. And you'll ask her to a movie, something sappy. She'll say, "I'd love to."

Weeks later, in a restaurant, she'll sit quietly across from you. While you're lost in the fact that you can hardly remember anything before her.

But that night,, there'll be something different in her eyes.

She'll say, "I have to tell you something." You'll wait, remembering another night long ago.

She'll hesitate, take a careful breath, and say, "I'm falling in love with you."

Your world will stop, then start again . . . and the steak will never taste better.

i never saw the leaves
(for gina)

i never saw the leaves as beautiful as this
i never knew the trees could somehow share our kiss
i never saw the rivers genuflecting to the sky
i never saw the leaves so sacred in good-bye
i never heard the sunset, I never knew its song
and in this dawn and morn' of autumn,
    somehow we belong
i never saw the cattails laughing in the wind
the birds all stop within their flight to ask us
    how we've been
i never saw the leaves as perfect as today
and i swear i heard them singing,
    i thought i heard them say
that they'd never known two people so very much in love
while orange-browns and golden-reds do frolic up above
i never felt the moonlight, so clean and filled with grace
its purple-silver halo surrounds this holy space
and in this dream of moonbeams, i take you in my arms
the willows sleep in wonder,
    the stars have all been charmed
i never knew october so full of sweet surprise
the green that fades upon the trees still breathes
    within your eyes
same trees do blush before our love
    and gently bow to kiss
i never saw the leaves as beautiful as this

questions

what moments of love do you most remember in your life?

what are the greatest acts of love you've ever seen?

is it really better to have loved and lost than never to have loved at all?

have you been taking someone you love for granted?

list three reasons someone would love you.

part four

to borrow
a child's
eyes

~

Amid the storm,
there is only
the color of
your son's hair.
—Hugh O'Neill

life doesn't offer many second chances. In fact, many times, it doesn't even give us one shot at the brass-and-foil ring.

That's why it would be crazy to ignore the second chance that comes through children. Whatever our relationship is to them, whether we're parents, family, friends, or mentors, they are sacred teachers. And that's good because, as always, we have so very much to learn.

Much to learn of life's glory, found in their stories of courage and compassion. And just as much to learn in the darker places, like grief and anger, those alleys we don't dare walk alone.

So, listening to children brings second chances. It allows us to see the world new through their eyes. As we struggle into our boots and gloves and rush out the door into a first snow. As we run into our mother's arms crying, asking her to kiss the finger we just hurt, simply knowing her kisses can heal.

And listening to children makes us remember our fears. Like worrying about the school bully who promised he'd find us after school. Or lying helpless and sleepless in our bedroom, waiting for the boogeyman to come out of the closet once our parents say goodnight and close the door.

All of it. Waiting for us to learn it again through children or as children to our parents. Because, just as we are taught, we teach, giving our parents second chances to work it out, to get things right that they might have gotten wrong.

Second chances offer a gift. One that allows us to apply our adult minds, hearts, and experiences to what we see again through a child's eyes. To learn the lessons we couldn't have learned the first time around.

A gift that helps us see a sunrise as more than just another chance to make a buck. That stops us from quickly turning the newspaper page showing the refugee who grieves. That inspires us to give someone a second chance, someone who needs nothing more than a cupful of forgiveness and a tablespoon of grace.

In this section, then, I share with you my children and the world they've given me through their words, their actions, and the way they believe. Jeremy, Matthew, and Alexandra.

I share stories of becoming and being a parent. Of the days when I search bookshelves for tips on raising children, desperately seeking advice on how to help them believe in themselves and their power to change the world.

Of the nights when I feel like a child in a man's body, having little idea of how to be a parent and wondering how I'm ever going to learn by the morning. But, lying there, I begin to understand that we're not expected to be perfect; we're just expected to try.

Then, the sun rises again. And with it, a second chance . . . and a third . . . and a fourth . . .

the journey begins

Most people return from Las Vegas with winnings or souvenirs. My wife came back with a baby.

After loading Gina's suitcases into our van at the airport for the ride home, my wife handed me a small package. Thinking it would be a wonderfully tacky souvenir, I ripped through the paper only to come face to face with a positive pregnancy test.

Now my wife and I had been trying to have another baby for quite some time. So, when I saw the test, my first thought was, *What the heck is this?* Not very poetic, unfortunately, but very much the truth.

So, I immediately looked up to find my wife smiling.

"But how?" I mumbled, knowing exactly how but not when or where.

"I was sicker than you'll ever know in Vegas," Gina whispered, so as not to let on yet to our boys in the backseat. "So my mom took me to a doctor. And, with all the other tests, they wanted to make sure I wasn't pregnant. But I guess I am."

Another baby. A third boy? A first girl? A thousand thoughts and feelings ran through me.

I'm happy. And scared. And worried that I won't be a good enough dad. And proud of "big brother" Jeremy. And nervous that Gina and I'll now be outnumbered. And sad for Matthew that he'll no longer be the baby. And hoping we'll be able to make them all feel special.

And, most of all, so in awe of my wife who, once again, will show how a woman is a miracle, how she brings forth life and beauty and peace into a world so dearly in need of all three.

I write about the meaning in moments. There aren't many to top hearing that there's a baby on the way.

The journey begins . . . again.

she became amazing

Last night, Gina and I were lying in bed, reading pregnancy books, to learn more about our unborn baby.

Now, for me, one of the greatest challenges during pregnancy is figuring out how far along we are. Because there are about fourteen different ways to tell how many weeks old the baby is. One begins at conception. Another has to do with "womanly" stuff (that's as far as I'm going with that). Then, of course, one is somehow linked to the duration of the arctic summer and mortgage rates.

So, as far as I can tell, we are in our 4,362nd week.

Afterwards, I put my mouth against Gina's stomach and talked to our child. Now having a conversation with a fetus is not easy. In fact, it can be pretty difficult to find common ground. So I usually start with something about the European balance of power and then put my hand on her to see if the baby responds.

And that's when it happened! Nineteen weeks into my wife's pregnancy, I felt the baby move. And, although I've gone through this before, it's never the same. Because feeling our baby move lets me know yet again that there are things here in this world of ours that can't be categorized, photocopied, or lectured upon.

And my wife, who is once again a mother, has become a world to our unborn child.

The only planet she or he has ever known.

the other sock

I wasn't worried until the contractions were five minutes apart.

Gina hadn't been feeling well. But I had no idea that we'd be driving to the hospital at 1:30 in the morning, a full six weeks before our baby was due.

It started innocently enough, with Gina saying simply that her stomach hurt. But soon, we noticed that her "stomachaches" were coming every ten minutes.

And, although we've had other children, I immediately became the zany sitcom expectant dad, hurriedly packing a bag, without any idea of the contents. In fact, it's only now that I realize I packed one sock, four pairs of underwear, and my *Consulting for Dummies* book.* You know, just in case I had to consult in my underwear during the delivery.

Then, driving to the hospital, I began to understand that we might soon be holding our third child. And that's when I prayed for courage and confidence in the face of being a dad again. After all, who am I to raise a child when I can't even pack a hospital bag?

Fortunately, those thoughts faded as we pulled up to the emergency room. There, the doctor determined that, although her contractions were only three minutes apart, Gina wasn't ready to give birth. So they gave her fluids and medication and we enjoyed for a refreshing half-hour of sleep.

---

* *Consulting for Dummies* by Bob Nelson and Peter Economy (Hungry Minds, Inc., 1997).

That's it. Just a false alarm. A common story, indeed. But it's going to be the real thing, soon. And when it is, I hope I pack the other sock.

into our hands

She's beautiful.

Yesterday, Gina and I went to the doctor, thinking we'd be back home within a few hours.

Five hours later, after Gina had been through contractions that I would have run screaming from, she was ready to push.

As she began, our doctor asked me how much I wanted to do. At first, I didn't understand what he meant, but then I realized that he wanted to know how big a role I wanted to play in the delivery. So, quickly, I answered, "Everything."

After I answered, he told me to put on a pair of gloves. Instead of moving, though, I stood stunned, just beginning to realize that I was going to be more involved than I ever imagined. Luckily, a nurse helped me struggle into the gloves and I was ready.

The doctor then called me over and positioned me to deliver the baby. And, as Gina pushed, I looked up at her and realized that she was having our baby and I was helping bring our baby into the world—and there just aren't many moments like that.

As Gina pushed, the doctor guided me with his voice and hands. "Left, now down, up, now down again, be careful with the head, okay, we're almost there, watch the shoulder." Then silence, as our baby daughter was born into my hands. Silence for only seconds, until she began to cry.

Alexandra Marie Warda was born on September 24, 2000 at 2:05 p.m. She was 7 pounds, 13 ounces, and 20 inches long.

A daughter. I'm in deep, serious trouble.

when angels play
with alexandra

There was something in Alexandra's eyes.

A neighbor came over this week to drop off a present for our new baby daughter. As we talked, I let her hold Alexandra, who had fallen asleep after a good cry in Dad's arms. Then, as she slept, Alexandra smiled.

Our neighbor, seeing this, whispered, "When babies smile, it means an angel is playing with them."

And, as always, moments connect.

Because earlier that day, I had been holding my daughter, looking into her eyes. Into eyes looking directly back at me, unflinching, and so conscious. Into eyes that held some divine secret, a tender tale about where she had been before she was born. As if she had witnessed a mystery so beautiful that she wanted nothing more than to share it.

But, as you know, newborns can't talk. Almost as though that secret isn't meant to be shared, only lived.

So, later, as our neighbor talked of angels, I thought back to what I had seen in Alexandra's eyes. The deep knowing and perfect compassion that looked out at me through her. And, most of all, the words, "You are loved."

In some ways, I was scared by what she showed me. But then, I remembered that when you're loved, it *can* make you uncomfortable. It *can* make you wonder what it is in you that inspires that type of devotion.

Somehow, though, I didn't have those questions this time. Because it all made sense in Alexandra's eyes.

helpless

The nurse was taking blood from Matthew's heel. She'd first tried to find an artery in his arm but, like me, his arteries tend to hide when confronted with steel. So, after looking for several more minutes, she said, "I'll have to take it from his foot."

And right then, I knew I was about to learn another lesson. Because no matter how much you hurt me, you can't hurt me more than by hurting my children. Even if it is for their own good.

And the lesson began simply enough, with the knowledge that love makes its demands.

Starts out cute and cuddly, with yellow balloons and blue crepe paper. Smiles its winning smile and keeps saying that life will be grand. But then, after love's been around for a while, and has its own razor and toothbrush in your bathroom, and its favorite radio stations programmed into your stereo, that's when things begin to get ugly.

Because that's when love demands sacrifice. Plops itself down in the middle of you and says, "Okay, you thought you knew what love was. Well, guess what? I'm gonna need you to suffer a little here. And it's going to get worse before it gets better. In fact, let's start right now with your baby son. How about if you hold him while a nurse jabs his heel with a needle. Then she'll milk the skin to get enough blood to fill a tube. How's that? Can you handle it? Or will you run?"

I had no answer.

Instead, I simply held Matthew tighter. With the nurse squeezing his heel, hoping to not need to stick him again. And he cried, while looking back and up at me as if to say, "Dad, why? Why are you letting them do this? I thought you were supposed to protect me, not hold me down while someone hurts me."

But I didn't look away, although I felt helpless. My son was in pain and there was nothing I could do—but I would be there for him.

Finally, the nurse finished and left the room. I sat quietly, holding my sniffling son, wiping his tears with my sleeve. As I did, I realized that I had never expected to feel so sad just holding him for a blood test. In fact, it shook me and left me trembling.

Later, as we drove home, with Matthew contemplating his sucker, I replayed the visit in my head to find the lesson. What was I being taught?

Then, like lightning, I knew. I was supposed to see that I wouldn't be able to fix everything, that sometimes I would, indeed, be helpless to keep my children from suffering. But, in those moments, I would need to be strong.

Yes, love makes its demands. And when it does, sometimes the only answer we have is just being there.

so sweet forgiveness

I found sweet forgiveness in my son's arms.

Every morning, I wake up and hope that I'll get this dad thing right. Keep thinking that I'll finally learn patience and wisdom. But it's a struggle.

Like last night, when I came home, beaten down by the quickest thrills of dollar bills that promise bigger houses and faster cars. When the first thing I saw in the doorway was Jeremy's backpack on the floor.

So I yelled, "Jeremy! Come here!"

After I did, he came slowly into the room, looking sad and a little scared because how else are you supposed to look when someone bigger controls much of your life.

"Sorry, Dad," he mumbled, and walked away with backpack in hand.

But later, after Gina tucked him in, I walked into his room and sat on his bed. He looked up tentatively, as if expecting to be reprimanded again, and that hurt most of all.

So I bent down, kissed his cheek, and whispered, "Jeremy, I'm sorry. I wasn't a very good dad tonight. I'm just tired, but that's no excuse."

And with that, he hugged me and said, "That's okay, Dad, I love you."

I wish you that kind of love.

sometimes, you have to break the rules

Never buy Baltic.

I should have known it was going to be a long night. After all, I was washing the dishes when I heard Jeremy yell, "Dad, you're going to be the thimble." Unfortunately, I had my heart set on the race car. Possibly the dog. But the thimble? Could a man use the thimble and still be cool?

"All right, I'll be the thimble, but I want to be the banker, too."

"No way," Jeremy replied. "Mom's the banker. She's better at being the banker."

What? My wife, a better banker? All right, so I once had a little trouble with geometry, but this was the ultimate indignity—my son telling me that I couldn't even handle the fiduciary responsibility demanded by Monopoly.

Soon, we were ready. The money was stacked in perfect rows and the dice sat expectantly. Each of us eyed the board, scheming. And as we did, we coveted.

Jeremy wants Boardwalk, always has. For Gina, it's the reds—Illinois, Indiana, and Kentucky. Me—well, give me the purples and oranges and I'm fine. I've learned to get a monopoly quick, build responsibly (following all municipal and environmental guidelines, of course), and slowly bleed my opponents dry.

The problem was that on this night, we were playing by "Jeremy's Rules." Yes, every few weeks, we play a game according to whatever rules Jeremy makes up.

And with Monopoly, Jeremy's rules go something like this. He's the car. I'm the thimble. His mom's the cowboy on the horse. In the beginning, he gets extra $500s. If he lands on a utility, he gets $500. If we land on a utility, we go to jail. If he lands on a railroad, he gets $500. If we do, we go to jail.

Of course, he gets free property to start the game. My wife and I get the honor of letting him roll first . . . second . . . and third. We can't buy Boardwalk or Park Place. If we do, we have to immediately give them to him, especially if he helped clean up after dinner. We can't ask for rent, can't buy houses, and always end up in jail. In the meantime, if he feels like it, he gets $500.

As you might have guessed, with "Jeremy's Rules," Jeremy tends to win.

The thing is that, at first, when we're not playing by the official rules, I get uncomfortable. Because it's hard for me to let go, to not point at the directions on the box and say, "Jeremy, you cannot be three pieces at once!"

But, after awhile, I notice that we're laughing more. And it strikes me that it's fun to sometimes break the rules. As long as nobody's getting hurt, it's quite a relief to just do what you feel. Best of all, children seem to know that inherently.

The game continued. After Jeremy owned most of the board, though, I made the fatal mistake of buying Baltic to finish off my lone monopoly. I bought hotels. I thought I could fight my son's domination. But I was horribly wrong.

The last thing I remember was handing over my last $5. And with a casual flick of his finger, my thimble flew off the board. But, as they say, if you're gonna break the rules, you have to break a few hearts along the way.

letting go

Over the weekend, I was helping Matthew learn to walk. As I did, he stumbled in front of me, with his arms stretched above his head and each hand grasping my fingers.

After a time, though, I wanted to sneak my hands away, hoping he would walk on his own. So, first, I took away my left hand. When I did, he complained but soon was walking confidently, like John Travolta at the beginning of *Saturday Night Fever*.

Then I pulled away my right hand. At this indignity, Matthew began to whimper, looking back up at me as if he had been betrayed.

But as much as I wanted to, I didn't give in. I let him balance his "Weebles Wobble" body against me but refused to give him a supporting hand unless he at least tried to walk. At the same time, however, I crouched down and kept my arms on each side of him in a protective circle, ready to catch him.

Realizing that he could either continue to complain or try to walk, he tried and made two steps before falling. Luckily, though, my arms were there and I righted him.

And, at that moment, it struck me that I'd be doing this for Matthew for the rest of his life. Not physically, of course. He would soon be walking on his own.

But emotionally, spiritually, and morally, I'll walk behind him, with my "arms" encircling but not touching him, not interfering with his will, yet helping him stand and telling him that he can most certainly do it.

And I'll be there if he should fall. When he tries and fails, I'll catch him. Not immediately, of course, because he needs to understand what has gone wrong and feel the consequences of what he has done. But before he hits the ground, my arms will be there.

Now, when he succeeds, I'll use those same arms to hug him while I say, "I knew you could."

And even when I'm gone, I'll be there. To help my children stand *then* by teaching them *now*. And those teachings will become my arms.

My loving arms around them . . . just in case.

"needs improvement"

I grade myself as a parent. Last night I got a D minus.

I grade myself. Not formally and not every night. But frequently, just before falling asleep, I'll grade how I did as a dad that day.

If I held my sons, laughed deep, and made them feel special, I get an A. If they know without a doubt that they mean the world to me, I get an A plus.

If I spent time with my boys, laughed some, or played a game, that usually brings a B. If I sat with them but talked on the phone or read the newspaper, a C for sure. Because, what's worse—to not be there or to be there and still be gone?

So last night, I came home tired and worn with the world clinging to me like an angry octopus. Jeremy was excited that I was home and Matthew had just woken up. Yet, I had forgotten how much the two boys on the other side of the door needed me.

Because this too-much-with-the-world man was in desperate need of a new mood.

You see, Jeremy is five and he does five-year-old things like spilling milk and forgetting to pick up toys. So when I walked in, I thought a tornado had spent the day in the house. Plus, Matthew was teething *and* hungry—not the best combination.

So I put on sweats, hoping that taking off business clothes would improve my attitude. Like taking off a shirt after the bar, hoping the smell of smoke would fade. It didn't. I was still tired and didn't have time for my boys. Ashamed to write it but it's true.

Then I snapped at everything Jeremy did. When I put Matthew in his crib, he cried until I grudgingly picked him up.

So when Jeremy yelled that he wanted to play a game, I yelled right back, "Jeremy, I'm trying to take care of your brother—don't be so selfish!" Of course, I should have just walked down the stairs and out of the house right then because I clearly wasn't doing this father thing well at all.

By the end of the night, though, I had fixed things a bit. First, I read a book about trucks to an exhausted but not-yet-ready-for-bed Matthew. As I did, I studied his face and tiny hands, and knew that part of me would go on.

Then I held Jeremy. He asked me to tell him about the movie I'd just bought him, *King Kong Versus Godzilla*. I did, leaving out the scariest parts, of course, ending with King Kong winning but still caring deeply about Godzilla's feelings.

In bed later, I silently relived the night and thought, "D minus would be about right." I was just glad that I'd have another chance the next day. And, this time, I promise—I'll study harder.

i borrow my sons' eyes

This morning, I stood at the window, glaring at snow. Lots of it. More than I wanted to see on a winter Monday. "Damn," I muttered. "I've got to drive through this?"

I knew there was more there, though. More than how it appeared. Even possibly a lesson. So I walked into my five-year-old's room on 6:00 a.m. feet. Without the light. I didn't want to wake Jeremy. I just needed his eyes.

Again, I looked out the window, but this time, with Jeremy's eyes. Amazing, the difference. Evergreens turned into ghosts. Patio furniture became medieval winter castles.

Then, Matthew's eyes also brought the new. I saw as only a ten-month-old can see. White chunks of sky fell. My fingers traced spaghetti lines through a wet window. What was a window anyway? Nothing there, but it stopped my hands.

You see, whenever I forget the sacred, I borrow my sons' eyes. Jeremy sees giant robots where I see only electrical towers. Matthew can stare at a ceiling fan for hours with a jack-o'-lantern smile.

Later, in the car, I drove first with my eyes. Everyone in my way and too slow. "Speed up!" I yelled at a five-mile-per-hour person, oblivious to the fact that my windows were closed. The snow was quicksand as my wipers frantically tried to stay ahead of the storm.

Then, through my sons' eyes again. To the right, a forest, brilliant white. Each tree branch was cotton-tipped. And, although I could see only a short way in, I knew that if I walked into that place, I'd find myself in a land of elves and dragons and silver-green rivers.

And when I looked to the left, a stream slept at the bottom of a hill, like black wrinkled cellophane. It knew I watched.

At work, I crunched my way to the door. As I opened it, though, I caught my reflection in the glass. And there I saw my face and a knowing smile. Because I had borrowed my sons' eyes.

wrapped around her finger

I've seen the future—and its name is "Barbie."

With our new daughter, I find myself knee-deep in revelations every day. For instance, there's Barbie. And my first halting steps down the Barbie aisle at the toy store as I discover her stuff. So much of it. Like planes, cars, motorcycles, condominiums, pools, horses, spas, kitchens, computers, and on and on and on.

And other stuff, like designer clothes, jewelry, shoes, makeup, and accessories. With more fashion options than real women have at almost the same price!

I don't get it.

Then, a second revelation, when I open Alexandra's closet. Because, although she's only eleven weeks old, it's filled to bursting!

And that's because everyone brings her an outfit. Even people we don't know stop by to give her clothes. As they do, I wonder why they didn't do the same when my boys were born. But when I ask, Gina just looks at me, sighs, shakes her head, and walks away.

Because I just don't get it.

So it's slowly dawning on me that I don't quite get it and have much to learn. That my little girl is going to take me on a journey. And that, although I may leave enough kisses on her cheeks to outnumber the stars, she'll still have the power to turn my world upside down.

By the way, did I tell you I also worry about her wedding? About how I'll cry when I walk her down the aisle, remembering her sleeping in my arms? Or how I'll feel when her new husband kisses her after he puts a ring on her finger?

But for today, I'll just let the revelations wash over me. With so very much to learn while the only thing wrapped around Alexandra's finger is me.

he has my heart

"Jim, they're treating our department like a red-headed stepchild."

I was sitting in a morning meeting when a co-worker used these words. A simple five-word phrase I'd heard many times before, but one that always hurts. Because, you see, I happen to have a stepson.

As the meeting continued, I thought more about the phrase "like a redheaded stepchild" and how it's used so easily. But, also, how I had never seen anyone confronted with how much pain that phrase can cause.

Obviously, the man across the table had no idea that the words could be offensive. If he had, I knew him as someone who would rather die than hurt my feelings. However, I didn't think I should stop the meeting and point out that you can't tell a man is a stepfather just by looking at him.

Now, I knew that he was using the phrase to explain that he thought our department was being shortchanged by the company. For him, in fact, the phrase was merely a way of describing how it feels to not be treated as well as someone else.

But that's where the problem comes in. Because the phrase implies that a stepchild is less than a biological child, someone a parent can like, and possibly love, but never to the same degree as his or her own child.

And, as I came to that realization, I went back in time to the day when Gina, Jeremy, and I got married. When I stood at the front of the church, waiting as she and Jeremy walked down the aisle into the weave of my life.

Since then, I have had very little use for the word "stepson." Not that I'm ashamed of the word, which has its uses, but because, for me, there's very little reason to describe Jeremy as anything but my son. And, since our wedding day, he has become even more.

Because I have sat with him on fever-filled nights, feeling the helplessness that parents know when they can do little else but hold their child.

Because I learned to become a dad when I still wasn't sure how to be a man, looking in amazement at the back-seat of my car where a child's car seat and diaper bag replaced softball bats and compact discs.

Because, although the courts don't often listen very much to stepparents in legal matters, I will fight until my last breath to be noticed.

Because I have answered his questions about girls and sex while looking everywhere but his eyes, not knowing how much I should say and whether or not I was using the right words.

Because when Matthew, my second son, was born, we were amazed by how much he and Jeremy looked alike. And, when Jeremy held him in the hospital room, they were forged so tight that there wasn't enough space between his arm and Matthew's cheek for a word like "half" to enter.

Because parents are made by what they do each day, by showing up at Little League games and school plays, by bandaging cuts and pushing swings, and by pretending they're sleeping so their children can scare them.

Because when Jeremy hands me a Father's Day card, it means just as much as if he were my biological son. In fact, it means something else, too. Because I chose him. I made the decision to bring him into my life, to take on the responsibility of raising him, of helping him become true and brave and willing to stand for what needs to be stood for.

And isn't that what love is? Being there through the hard times, when it would be so much easier to turn away, saying, "Well, it's been fun," and walk out the door to a simpler—but lonelier—life.

But the moment I married Gina and Jeremy, I made a promise. A promise that I'd always be there, that I would do my best to make them proud, and that, from that day on, Jeremy would be my son.

That is why I will speak up the next time the phrase "like a redheaded stepchild" is used. Because, first of all, I know many fine redheaded people. And, second, and most of all, I know one little boy who, although he may not share my blood, most definitely has my heart.

baby's home journal

While going through my baby son's things, I discovered that he's been keeping a journal. In fact, here's his entry for one day last week:

5:33 a.m.: Cry, hoping Dad will wake up and get me out of this crib. Diaper's wet. Not happy.

5:35 a.m.: Back to sleep for ten minutes to fool Dad, who's now awake and listening to the monitor.

5:45 a.m.: Cry again—this time, louder. Dad will have just gotten back to sleep so this'll be great!

6:17 a.m.: Realizing I mean business, Dad will come in to pick me up with crazy hair and sleep-deprived eyes. But then I'll give him my patented "Aren't-I-the-cutest-thing-on-the-face-of-the-earth?" smile. He'll never know what hit him.

6:43 a.m.: Mommy's feeding me waffles. And Cheerios. And whatever else comes within my reach.

8:27 a.m.: Dad and I are playing trucks. I ram the fire engine into his foot to hear those new words.

10:14 a.m.: My brother and I are watching "Blues Clues," a highly interactive and entertaining show. And isn't my vocabulary amazing?

12:12 p.m.: Lunchtime! Oops, bit Mom's finger. With my teeth. I'm dangerous on the dance floor! But she can't help but smile through the pain. Cause I'm so cute!

12:46 p.m.: Outside. In my wagon and they're taking pictures again. They're always taking pictures of me. I feel like Cher.

1:42 p.m.: Sleepy. Head down on Dad's shoulder. He, of course, thinks he's died and gone to heaven.

2:12 p.m.: In my crib. What's the deal with that? Who gave them the right to determine when I take naps? I was perfectly content talking to my Fisher-Price lawn-mower and they put me up here. Well, I'll show them. Wait until they get a load of this diaper.

3:21 p.m.: Wake up. Try to see how many toys I can get in my mouth. Easier when I drool. I guess the lubricatory effect of the drool is highly effective.

5:07 p.m.: Dinnertime! Mommy's trying to fake me out by putting rice under a piece of bread. I hate the feel of rice on my tongue so I'll stubbornly keep my mouth closed and wait her out. I always win!

6:14 p.m.: Bath time. Dad turns on the water and I get so excited, dancing around yelling. Then I slap the water, shove a washcloth in my mouth, and see how many toys I can throw out of the tub.

7:16 p.m.: I do believe I'm tired again. I can always tell 'cause everything gets a little fuzzy and out of focus and people's voices start to echo. Either that or I've been to a Pink Floyd concert.

7:44 p.m.: Falling asleep on Mommy's shoulder just might be the best thing in the world. Jeremy and Daddy already kissed me and told me to sleep well.

7:52 p.m.: Mommy kissed me goodnight and turned out the light. I sure do love my family. Well, sleep tight. And if any of you out there have a baby or know a baby, be careful what you say around them. They might just be keeping a journal like me.

i saw the light

At the holiday light show, I crossed over that jagged gray line between youth and what comes after.

It began during my family's annual visit to the "Winter Wonderland" near our house, where a mansion and its grounds are decorated for Christmas, with hundreds of light displays, music, and carloads of good cheer.

As in the past, we took the minivan. Just me, Gina, and the children, on a December night. The van was my second tentative footstep over that gray line.

The first step over it had been marriage, over three years before, to my wife and her son. And, on that day, my vow had included the line, "I promise to love, honor, and cherish you, although I will never *ever* buy a minivan." But, as they say, the best laid plans . . .

As in past years at the light show, Gina and the children wore pajamas. It was my wife's idea. For her, it meant being cozy and warm. For me, it was fine, as long as I didn't have to do it.

But this year, something *was* different. Something simple but momentous. Because this year, I was in pajamas, too! Yes, me. The final pounding footfall into adulthood.

I don't know how it happens. One day you meet a woman and fall in love. A love that turns your world downside up and tears the breath from your lungs. The next day you're driving a minivan in your pajamas. And you're scared.

And I was. Because even though I'm a grown man and a father, it's difficult to admit that I am now responsible for taking care of my wife's heart and helping shape our children into adults.

So, with those thoughts, I paid the entrance fee, turned off my headlights, and slowly drove into the wonderland.

"Dad," Jeremy joked, pointing to the first display on an arch over the road. "Look out! There's a reindeer jumping over the car."

"Minivan," I corrected him, half hearing his annual warning, still lost in thought.

Because I was in my pajamas. What if someone saw me? What if the guys I played touch football with happened to be around? Luckily, though, it was dark.

After a few more minutes of worrying, I looked back to see Matthew entranced by the dance of lights, as they took form in animals, castles, and elves. Alexandra slept the sleep of an angel.

Farther on, Santa filled his sleigh with presents. Then toy soldiers carefully guarded a castle as Jeremy's head turned side to side, not wanting to miss a bulb.

As I drove, I again considered my predicament. Yes, I was driving a minivan. And, yes, I was in my pajamas. But what was so wrong with that? After all, the truth is that I *am* an adult. I'm *not* a kid anymore.

Now, my children are the kids and I'm the father and that's the way it's supposed to be. And, at some point, it *is* time to put away the things of a child while keeping the childlike qualities that keep us young.

Then I looked around once more at my family, and something inside me shifted up and slightly to the left. As it did, everything became sacred. And, in a sweet flash, it hit me. The song "Circle of Life" came to mind, as I understood that I'd crossed over completely into adulthood and accepted my new place in life. A place where a jagged gray line turns into the distinct outline of a pajamed man in his minivan.

the man behind
the curtain

Like the Wizard of Oz, I'm not always what I appear to be. For instance, you're probably thinking I'm a loving husband and dad.

Well, lately, I'm not so sure.

Because I've been making my way toward my purpose. A purpose to tell me and you that one by one by one we're connected by moments.

But at the same time, I have a full-time job that makes me a part-time dad. Someone who tells his children that he can't play with them because he's too busy writing about what they mean to him.

A loving husband who often comes home tired and angry from searching for his way. In the front door like Godzilla, crashing and smashing through dinner, then disappearing upstairs to write, while his wife wonders what happened to the man she married.

And that's when I struggle to be loving, good, and brave. But it's so hard, and I sometimes feel beaten, unable to figure out what the next step could be.

So what do you do when you write about love but end up bitter at the end of the day? How do you reconcile the fact that you're not what you hoped to be, a man of courage who would split the sun just for the chance to be true?

And the only answer I come back with is that, no matter what, I will try to be a better man, each day, for my wife, my children, my family and friends, and, of course, for you.

Because, as far as I know, that is the only real way back to Kansas.

just for you

My mom always said, "I wish my kids were young again!"

When she would say that, I'd answer with a nod and "I know." But I didn't know. Because I didn't have children.

Now that I do, though, I get it. And I'd like to publicly apologize to my mother for not realizing how hard it is to watch your children grow up as you want nothing more than for them to stay little.

Yes, it's probably a bit selfish. But it also says something definite about love. Because the job of parents is to help their children become independent. But this forces parents to learn another difficult lesson—letting go.

I'm intimately familiar with this lesson because my children have been growing up quite a bit lately. The moments have been wonderful and sad all at the same time because I know my children will never be little again.

One such moment came at a restaurant yesterday. As we walked to our table, the host asked if we'd need a high chair. I was about to say "Yes" when Gina quickly answered "No." When she did, I looked over in surprise until I remembered that Matthew had recently begun sitting in a regular chair. And I realized that Matthew had moved into another stage of life. As I did, my heart ached for him to be a baby again.

Yes, Mom, I understand only too well.

Looking back, I've noticed other signs, too. Such as packing away their baby clothes. Sitting there, going through sleepers, shoes, and underwear, amazed that your children were ever so small.

Or when they start saying words the right way. "Brgr peece!" becomes "Burger, please!" You're bittersweet as their cute fumblings become real communications.

Or, worse, when they start talking about boyfriends or girlfriends. Be still, my heart.

The scary thing is that I have no control over this. My children keep growing up. To fight the fleeing, though, I sometimes hold them close and study them so that, later, when they're older, I'll remember.

I look at their faces. Their noses and cheeks. Their eyes and lips. The full and glorious details of each of them.

And, as I do, there are so many feelings. Because, with each new thing they do, there's something they won't do any longer. Something that will simply become another stone in the road that makes their path.

Mom, I finally get it. And you know what. If I could, I'd be a child again, just for a moment, and just for you.

every precious second*

My life's changing. And it scares me . . . as change can do.

I'm getting older, watching my children grow as neighborhood kids call me "Mr. Warda," and knowing that life happens in a heartbeat. Unfortunately, this knowledge tends to make me less daring, a little less willing to upset the proverbial applecart, to put myself on the line or try something new.

And maybe that's why the leaves called to me as my wife and I picked apples at an orchard near our house. They began softly, then grew louder, until finally, on our way back to the car, they were almost deafening, at least to me.

"Do you hear them?" I yelled to Gina.

"Who?" Gina replied, in a normal tone.

"The leaves! Can't you hear them?" I repeated.

"Oh no," she said, almost to herself. "Are things talking to you again?"

Of course, Gina knows me well, knows that, from time to time in my life, things that can't talk sometimes do.

"Yes!" I answered, trying to block out the sound with a hand over one ear. "It's the leaves and, boy, are they loud!"

With that, Gina rolled her eyes and got into the car. After all, she is the long-suffering wife of a long-suffering writer who has been known to talk to snowflakes.

---

* Title inspired by del Amitri's song, "Opposite View." (del Amitri: waking hours, 1989, A&M Records). The song includes the lyrics, "Every precious second is a chance to change."

Before I got in, however, I looked back at the leaves again. And, as I did, they made one last attempt to get my attention by shouting three words. Three words that sent me spiraling back in time to moments when my children swam and walked straight through their fear of change.

First, I remembered taking Jeremy to a swim lesson. Watching as he swam confidently near the pool's edge, knowing that, at any moment, he could reach out for safety.

But then, his teacher moved him into the center of the pool and Jeremy's movements became erratic, with panic appearing on his face. Because, with the edge no longer in reach, he was in a strange place, with no way to orient himself. It was new, and it forced him to learn. But he soon began to swim smoother, until he no longer needed the edge.

Then the leaves threw me into a second memory, in which Matthew was just learning to walk. There he stood, unsure, at his toy box, looking back over his shoulder at his favorite toy, a light-up drum.

At first, he turned slowly, keeping one hand firmly on the box. Then he looked to me, pleading, reaching out for my hand. And, although it hurt me not to help, I wanted him to learn. After all, that's what dads are for.

Instead, I turned on his drum so that it lit up and played music, knowing that would make him want it more.

Finally, with baby legs turning awkwardly, he let go. And, with fearful, frantic steps, he reached the drum and toppled into my arms. As his reward, I gave him the toy, kissed his cheek, and whispered, "I'm proud of you."

Matthew had changed, let go of what he knew for what might be.

My children had faced their fears of change, had let go of the certain for the learning that only comes with risk. They had taught me well.

I remembered those moments as we drove home. And, as I did, I prayed once again for the type of courage my children showed.

For, change can terrify before it enlightens. Yet, change also calls. That push and pull. That tender tension. You can pretend you don't hear its voice. You can listen, instead, to the cool, clear sounds of stagnation. But you can't fool yourself.

So I'll never forget the leaves . . . or their three simple words. Words that taught me that, at every moment, I have a choice. To change or stay the same, no matter how ridiculously routine it all gets.

No, I'll never forget the leaves. Or the day they told me about "every precious second."

sounds a lot like love

I took my children Christmas shopping yesterday. While we walked through the last-minute sales and the earnest ho-hos of the mall Santa, it struck me that few people were smiling.

And I wondered if somehow, in the middle and midst of the holidaze, we hadn't misplaced the season.

Then Jeremy pulled at my coat and asked if I'd buy him a toy. As I had done at least five times before that night, I explained that we were there to buy for his mom. But, as children do, he waited a few minutes and asked again.

"Jeremy," I explained, impatiently, "sometimes, we have to put other people before ourselves. You remember, don't you? I told you about sacrificing. It means 'to make sacred.'"

And, with that, he turned his eyes up to mine and said, "Dad, that sounds like love."

Yes, it does, Jeremy. Quite a bit.

a promise broken

Someone once said, "The things you love, you give time to." If that's true, then my children must sometimes wonder how much I care.

You see, I worked late again last night. Now I know that's no big deal. After all, many people do it every day— some more than others. When the job calls for it, you stay.

But as I drove home, I remembered telling Jeremy that we'd play baseball after I got home from work. I remembered the smile, the spontaneous hug he gave me, and the way his eyes leapt when I told him. Eyes filled with everything good that comes from knowing your dad wants to be with you. Sadly, though, it was already too dark for baseball, and knowing that I'd broken a promise made it darker still.

As I pulled into the driveway, my headlights cut across the front window. On most nights, when I come home, my children run up and press their eager faces against the glass, straining to see if it's me. Then, Matthew, my two-year-old, jumps up and down, yelling "Daddy car!" But last night, the window was empty.

Still, I walked quickly to the door, hoping to see them. But as I went in, Gina was just walking down the stairs. As she got to the bottom, she sighed and said, "Oh, Matthew just went to sleep." And, with that sad knowing, my shoulders slumped.

Because one of my children was asleep. And I hadn't seen him in the morning before I left, so that meant I had just gone a full day without him. One day out of his life that I wasn't part of, a day in which I wouldn't watch him learn new ways to touch the world, and couldn't kiss the swirling hair on top of his head.

Now I'm not asking for sympathy. Like other parents, I work to provide good things for my children. And I know there are many parents who travel quite a bit for their jobs, who miss more than one day with their children. No, I know I've got it good. But I do want to talk about choices.

Because we make choices every day. We decide whether to get up or hit snooze. We decide how much we'll spend and how much we'll save. We decide to speak up about things that matter or remain silent. We decide how best to take care of our families.

And that's where my significant choice came yesterday—going home to my family or making sure a project got done so that I could take care of the family I wasn't going home to. I chose to stay.

The problem is that Matthew doesn't know why I'm gone. All he knows is that I'm not there. Granted, he's small, but what about Jeremy? He knows I have to work, but that doesn't mean much to a boy who's waiting at the window for Dad. Will he remember these nights and think I didn't care? Did he gather his toys around him and wait for my headlights? Did his head start to drop as sleep threatened his vigil? And will he wake, remembering that I didn't keep my word and stop believing that a dad's promise is always true?

After I heard that Matthew was sleeping, I went up to his room and walked quietly to his crib. As I looked in, I found him snoring. But, instead of leaving, I took a few minutes to just look at him, to take him all in, knowing that minutes become days, and days become years, and before you know it, your kids are sharing graduation smiles and "walking down the aisles."

Surprisingly, as I stood there, I began to cry. Because I'd missed a day of my son's life. And my other son and I had passed in the hall like phantoms. Why did I miss that day? Because I wanted to give them simple things like food, a home, clothes . . . college.

I worked late the other night. Not a big deal. Just something you do, part of the job. Everyone does it. I just hope that my boys understand. When I'm home, they know I care. But do they know I love them when I'm gone? Again, I ask—"Do they know?"

the birds and those crazy bees

My son has started asking me about the birds and the bees.

And he's only *six*!

I thought I was being a cool dad when I told Jeremy that he could come to me with any questions he had about girls.

You see, he'd been asking a lot about the differences between boys and girls. At first, when he did, I'd just laugh and agree that they were quite different—like the fact that I've never seen a woman use as much wrapping paper as a man.

But, as he continued to ask, I realized that he wanted real information.

So that night, after reading him a story, I asked Jeremy if he had any questions about girls that I could answer. He thought for a few seconds and, while he did, I imagined him asking horrifyingly graphic questions that would demand details I wasn't even sure I knew.

But after what seemed like a thousand years, he whispered, "If you kiss a girl and her lips are dirty, will your lips get dirty, too?"

Stunned by his innocence and the wonder of it all, I struggled to keep from laughing with relief. And then, in my mind, I saw my six-year-old son kissing a girl.

"Yeah, Bud, if she's got dirt on her lips and you kiss her, you might get some on your lips. But don't worry, you won't mind . . . if you like her. Just remember to always treat a girl well."

"But what if she hits me?" he asked.

"Never, ever hit a girl," I answered, stronger than I had intended, but wanting to drive home the point. "If a girl is mean to you, just walk away. But never hit a girl."

"Okay," he replied, not quite understanding but taking my word for it.

And, with that, we shared a long, comfortable silence, as we were just two guys talking about girls.

Then Jeremy broke the silence with his next question: "Dad, why are girls' bodies different from boys' bodies?"

. . . and I ran screaming into the night . . .

questions

what have children taught you about yourself?

what grade would you give yourself as a parent or mentor, if you are one? how could you improve your grade?

what sacred moments have you shared with children?

if you were a child right now, how would you see the world? what would be most important to you?

what do you most want to pass on to the children? not want to pass on?

part five

this house
of grief
has many rooms

~

*Death cancels
everything
but truth.*
—Author unknown

this house of grief has many rooms. Rooms I didn't
know existed until I stood over my father's body at the
hospital. Rooms I never wanted to enter because it meant
holding my mother as she whispered that he looked so
cold and asked why they couldn't cover him to keep him
warm.

Rooms so filled with memories that I choke back
tears whenever I remember his stories or the way he'd
"silly walk" to make us laugh. Rooms of regret when I
think about him asking me to stay just a little longer and
me answering, "Dad, I've got to get home with the kids."

Even though I had to, it kills me now to think of the extra minutes I could have spent with him.

Rooms of respect when I think about him as a young man in 1944, in a bomber over France, knowing that at any minute his plane could be blown apart.

And, finally, rooms of honor now that my life has become not only mine but his. Because I swear he's with me and I want nothing more than to make him proud. As a good friend said, "You'll carry him with you in the way you carry yourself." And, as my sister offered, "I feel his absence, but I feel his presence more."

But, sadly, he's still gone. Still gone when our baby daughter, Alexandra, was born. Still gone when we bought our house, when what I most wanted to do was have him walk through it with me to consecrate it with admiring looks and careful, callused touches. And, still, still gone when I wrote this book. A book that I will take to the cemetery and offer to him when it is finished. A final gift from a son to his father, who was also a writer.

And, still, grief has many rooms. For, since he died, I've been learning its house well, finding that it isn't just an event, something that disappears when the last car pulls out of the cemetery. Because grief goes on.

Just as it's become part of me, a deadly serious fact of life that means you'll never see that person again. As essential to my structure as my lungs. As critical to what I believe as my faith.

Because this grief also teaches as it weaves its way. An ally, a dark companion, who points to life, saying,

"There, don't miss it, because it will be gone too soon!" And, so, grief is also essential to finding the sacred.

That is why, in the following stories, we'll walk with grief, talk with it, learn the rhythm of its breath and the feel of its touch. Whether it's in the death of a parent, or in other parts of the house, where it's from a broken heart, the radio reports of another school shooting, contemplating a will, or the realization that a dream has died. No matter its name, no matter its taste, it's still grief.

So, with that resolved, let's continue on. Because all journeys go through dark places, because all hills wind down into valleys, and because, most of all, to do it any other way, somehow, would be wrong.

even the trees wondered

My dad wanted to say good-bye.

That was my first thought when he told me that he wanted to buy magnolia trees for my brother and me.

At the time, I was driving him downtown to the doctor. And, as usual, my dad had fallen asleep. Actually, since having bypass surgery, my dad tended to sleep whenever and wherever he was. But, also since the surgery, I'd noticed that there didn't seem to be much of my old dad left.

When we pulled into the parking lot, my dad slowly woke up, looked over, and said that he wanted to buy us magnolia trees. Now, obviously, he'd been dreaming. So, upon seeing my confusion, he added that he'd always wanted to plant one in his own yard but never had. Then, on the way up in the elevator, he said it again, insisting that he had to buy us those trees.

Hearing his words, I struggled to hold back the tears. Because, although I may have been wrong, it sure sounded like something a man would say who didn't think he'd be around much longer. As if he were preparing.

Later, standing next to him in the doctor's office, I could tell that he was worse. Could feel the fear coming off him as he waited for the doctor to finish his exam. To be honest, I was scared, too. After all, how does a son say good-bye to his dad?

The doctor pronounced him to be well. But my eyes saw differently, as I knew something essential in him was gone.

A few days later, my brother and I took my dad to a nursery, along with Gina and the boys. Once there, Gina walked with me as I pulled Matthew in his wagon. Meanwhile, Jeremy had his Godzilla figures attacking desperate cities at the feet of the peach trees.

While we walked, the wind kicked up memories and took me back to when I was eleven years old, with my father and brother in a nursery. When my dad moved sure and strong among fruit trees and pine in the summer sun, testing branches with huge hands, showing us how to choose healthy trees. And, when you're eleven, your dad is a giant.

But, on this day, my dad was weaker. And even the trees wondered if this were the same man.

In fact, when I looked back at him, it hit me again that life and love make their demands. Because, although my dad still walked among the trees, he was smaller. And, although our coats were off in the seventy-degree weather, his overcoat collar was pulled tight against his too-thin neck, and his hat was pulled down against his ears.

Soon, moving slower to accommodate my father, I noticed saplings and dying trees. I took in their message of life and death. And my dad was still the same, yet completely different.

With this message, I raced Jeremy through the nursery. When I caught him, I kissed him and held him and, for a moment, thought of when he would one day turn back and see me smaller, too.

Then I found the perfect tree. "Hey, Dad!" I yelled, "Here it is!"

As I did, I realized that the tree had become more. For I knew that I would soon plant it with my father watching. He would sit on the patio with his feet up, drinking lemonade, saying, "A little to the right." And, Jeremy would help me, with smaller gloves and determined eyes. I would plant the tree with my son as my dad did with me.

Then, when my dad was gone, I would see the tree grow stronger. The tree would become everything. When spring came, I would rejoice as each blossom was my father's smile. When winter neared, I would weep, as naked branches were my father's fingers.

Afterwards, the workers loaded the magnolia into my van. As they did, I held my youngest son to my father's face. Matthew reached out and brushed his hand against my dad's dry lips, and my dad laughed and kissed his grandson's cheek. Then he pulled away—but something remained, faint trails of a sacred something suspended in the air between them.

Driving away, I saw my dad move slowly toward his car, worn from the day. As I looked at him, growing smaller in the rearview mirror, the man he had become blurred with the man he was before.

Then, for the briefest moment, I caught my own reflection in the mirror. When I did, I realized that I was my dad and my dad was me. And that, no matter what, he would remain.

my dad died

My dad died yesterday.

My pager went off as Gina and I were driving home from a day together downtown. When I called back, my mother told me that my dad had fallen and was being taken to the hospital. He'd been suffering lately from a back injury and was weakened by past heart problems. But he'd fallen before, so I wasn't overly worried.

So, as Gina and I walked up the hospital driveway to the emergency room, I thought about how I'd cheer him up with a joke and the promise of a Popsicle. But then I noticed my brother-in-law Markus coming toward us. He'd been the first to reach my dad and held his hand while calling the paramedics.

As he walked up, I asked him where my dad was, hoping that they'd release him soon and let him go home. Markus didn't answer.

So I asked again. This time, he whispered, "He's gone."

Not knowing what he meant, I asked again, with a rising voice, "Where is he? What did they do with him?"

As if he couldn't stand the taste of those words again, he instead turned his eyes up into the rain. And I quickly realized that everything had changed, that my father was dead. And that all those times when I'd comforted others who'd lost loved ones, I never really knew what that pain was like.

Because my dad's gone. And, this week, we'll have the wake and funeral and somehow help my mother move through it and we'll tell our children how "Grandpa" isn't alive anymore but that he will always love them.

And, somehow, I'll try to figure out what to do about my dad being gone and my heart being broken.

My dad died yesterday. So why do I keep thinking he'll call me tonight?

reflections on a
week of grief

Reflections on a week of grief after my dad's death:

—Being held by my wife as my legs buckled when I first heard that my dad had died. I leaned hard on her love this week.

—Hearing my sister gently ask if I wanted any of my dad's clothes. Standing in his closet, touching his shirts and suits, smelling his cologne, and trapped in the clear and brutal knowledge that I'd never see him again.

—Delivering the eulogy, talking about my father's love of simple things like cantaloupe, poetry, and mowing the lawn. A love probably born from having faced death every day during the war.

—Attempting to retain composure during the wake, when what I most wanted to do was run to his casket, grip him by the shoulders, and demand that he wake up and stop scaring Mom.

—Watching my mother wake to her first sunrise without him after fifty-three years of marriage. Knowing that, in that waking, there would come a moment when she'd remember.

—Seeing Jeremy help me and the other pallbearers carry the casket and then cry in my arms.

—Sitting here tired and deeply sad, wondering why I didn't hug my dad longer and kiss him harder the last time

I saw him alive. And thinking back on our last conversation, trying to remember if I told him I loved him.

—Finally, feeling proud to be his son, knowing that it is my father's love of words and justice that burns in me.

one last father's day

I want to give my dad one last Father's Day gift. The gift of sharing a moment that defined him.

In 1944, he was a navigator in bombers based in England. One day, their target was an ammunitions dump surrounded by antiaircraft guns and enemy fighters near Paris.

Now, since my dad was the mission's lead navigator, all forty-eight planes followed his directions. But, after dropping their bombs, the ground disappeared in fog and rain, leaving them lost! But, since he was the navigator, he was the only one who knew they were.

As they flew on, my dad said that a "panic and fear gripped me" as he tried to figure out their coordinates. A fear that grew worse when a Canadian bomber group, also lost, wanted to follow them back to England. Before giving the group permission to join, though, the pilot in my father's plane asked my dad if he knew where he was.

And, at that moment, my dad's life was defined. Because, instead of giving in to the fear, he answered, "Yes." He answered "yes" because he had decided somewhere inside himself that there was no way to answer "no."

So he thought carefully and had the entire formation turn toward a location where, he thought, a huge battery of enemy antiaircraft guns was located. He did this because the guns were distinctly identified on the map, so if he saw their shell bursts, he would then know exactly where he was.

When the planes turned, the sky in the distance erupted with antiaircraft fire, letting my dad know where he was. As it did, my dad immediately gave directions to the entire group that would get them to England. All 448 men made it back safely.

After hearing that story years later, I told my dad that he was a hero. But he just shook his head and said that the real heroes were the men who didn't come back from the war.

He explained that, as he fought through that moment years before, he remembered words his uncle shared with him before the war: "Be the tiger." Words meaning that if someone has a choice between running away or taking action, they should take action.

As for me, on my first Father's Day without my dad, I want to live the rest of my life as the tiger.

So, who's with me?

what's in your boxes?

What would we find in your boxes?

Since my dad died, my family has been going through his boxes, organizing the life he left behind. And with each opened box, I learn more about him.

More about his passions, like poetry, music, and flamenco dancing.

More about his compulsions, like keeping documents, no matter how unimportant, for over forty years.

More about his caring, like letters sent from clients, thanking him for being there through difficult times.

More about how he loved us. Because in those boxes were cards we'd given him throughout his life and remembrances of his children's achievements.

And, it was then, standing silent over those boxes, as tears and dust mixed upon my face, that I wondered what my children would find in my boxes when I'm gone.

Would they puzzle over the clothes that I used to wear on stage when I played in a rock band?

Would they argue over who would keep the blue Plexiglas peace sign I bought at a garage sale?

Would they be amazed at how many pictures I had of their mom?

Would they remark at how odd it was that I loved reading, writing, and music, just like my dad?

And, most of all, as they looked at the stories I'd written, would tears and dust mix upon their faces as they realized how much I loved them?

What will be in your boxes?

real

I've been struggling with what to write. In fact, I must have written ten stories in my head before mentally crumpling them up. Because the simple fact is, I'm not sure where to go from here.

After all, what do I write after writing about my dad who died three weeks ago? How do I tell you about the wonder in the wind, or the fact that we can change the world, when all I want to talk about is how much I miss him?

Or how scared I was when, yesterday, for just a moment, I forgot what it was like when he was alive? When I couldn't quite remember how it felt to kiss his cheek or how he laughed.

So you can see my dilemma. After all, I originally wanted to inspire you. But then, when my dad died, I realized that I just want to be real.

And being real is not always inspirational, especially when I'm committed to sharing my grief. A house left dark and cold, with cobwebs near the ceiling and rats running the walls.

So where do we go from here? We'll see.

But wherever it is, I promise you one thing. It will be real.

a matter of life and death

I wonder if our baby will have my dad's laugh?

I never used to talk much about death. But since my dad died two months ago, I've been thinking more and more about how life and death are joined.

Like yesterday, when Gina, Matthew, and I took my mom to the cemetery. We stood to the side of my dad's grave as she quietly told him about his grandchildren and how badly she missed him.

More than anything, I wanted to hold her, but I knew that she needed to grieve. As the sorrow became almost too much to take, though, Matthew grabbed her leg and called her until she turned and kissed the top of his head. In death, there is life.

At the graveside, my brother's daughters had built a campfire out of sticks to "keep Grandpa warm," and painted a birdhouse that now hung from the tree above. In death, there is life.

Later, we stopped at a baby store, looking at strollers. As you'd expect, the store was full of anticipation and joy. And my dad will never see our new baby. In life, there is death.

So, as I walk through this house of grief, behind the door on the left is a nursery where soon my wife will be holding our new baby.

Because, in life there is death and in death there is life. And what I used to see as black and white has now become, as a good friend used to say, a million shades of gray.

it's delicious

"It's delicious."

Matthew usually uses these words after eating something he likes. But lately, he's been using them to describe special moments as well.

Like, this weekend when, after a long night of swimming, we sat around a fire. Just before falling asleep, Matthew raised his eyes to the fire, then to the quarter moon, and said, "It's delicious, Daddy."

And, of course, he's right. It's all delicious. Every thick and thin of it. Every branch on every tree in every field we drive by.

Especially, yesterday, when Gina and I celebrated five years of marriage. Five years of the sun, the sorrow, and the sweet touch of someone who knows where you most need healing.

She sat across from me at the restaurant, smiling and brutally beautiful. Behind her was a painting of an Italian street, one so real that it looked like she was there and I was there and all I wanted to do was kiss her.

As we talked, we reminisced about our wedding day, of getting ready, with her hair being done at her house and my dad and I searching for bow ties at mine. Then, after the stories, came tears, as we wished together that my dad could have been with us on our anniversary.

And, right then, just as we made that wish, we heard his favorite song over the restaurant's speakers. "Time to Say Goodbye" by Andre Bocelli, a song we both last heard at an Italian restaurant after my dad's funeral, sung by the owner in Dad's honor.

So, with that, Gina and I decided that it was my dad wishing us a happy anniversary and kissing us with his rough, loving lips.

Yes, it's all delicious.

d e a r   d a d :

Dear Dad:

I know it's been almost five months since you died. But it feels more like five years, and so much has happened that I wanted to share with you.

First, you have a new granddaughter. Her name's Alexandra Marie, and she is amazing. We call her the "Duchess" because she's obviously royalty.

But most of all, I wish you were here to hold her.

Also, I just signed my first book contract. It'll be coming out soon, and it's about finding the sacred in our everyday moments. I know how badly you wanted to publish your own books, the one about John Keats, whose poetry meant so much to you, and the other one, about being an air force captain during World War II, to honor those who didn't come back.

So, this book will be for you.

Oh, and we also moved. But it hurt to walk through the new house without you, to know that you would have taken your time in each room, commenting on the quality. And then we would have walked outside to see my trees. Outside was where you most liked to be.

And when I mow the lawn now, I think of you the whole time.

Dad, so much has changed since you died. And it feels like a hundred years since I kissed you or hugged you or simply told you I love you.

I miss you, Dad. We all do.

Love, Jim

cemeteries are
sacred teachers

There are lessons to be learned among worn head-stones and autumn graves. Lessons of love, faith, and truth. And, most of all, the lesson that we will not always be here.

I first saw the lessons as a child. When my mother and I would visit her parents' graves. On the way, we'd buy flowers. Just enough so my mother might find some peace. Just enough to help her say, "I miss you."

And each year it would take forever to find their graves. Mostly because the only map we had was printed on my mother's heart. But after awhile, we'd come upon their headstones, each of marble with a photograph.

A faded black-and-white photograph of each of them. Her mother and father held there. I'd look down at my grandparents who I never met, and I'd wonder how I should act. Should I cry? After all, most people I'd seen at cemeteries cried. Or should I just be quiet?

The thing is, I didn't feel either way. Instead, I felt joy. After all, I was there on a perfect fall day, at my mother's side, as she tenderly cared for her parents' graves. Even as a little boy, I knew the unmistakable signs of love.

Today, I also find lessons in cemeteries. Lessons I want to pass on to my boys. So my wife and I sometimes take them to a cemetery, to walk and learn.

Like last week, when we pulled up on a gravel road at a cemetery near our house. A place where the line between this world fades into the mystery of the next.

Jeremy and Matthew were bundled against October as Gina held their hands. I walked with my notebook, listening. And, as I knew they would, the lessons came.

Lessons of courage as I saw a soldier's grave. Lessons of life where a baby was buried close to her father, forever in his arms. Lessons of love on a couple's headstone that told of how they would always be "living, loving, laughing, together, forever."

Lessons of peace, as so many headstones held the words "at rest." Words that reminded me that life is often hard and sometimes much too full of suffering and loss. Lessons of friendship on another headstone that read, "Erected by friends and fellow workmen," which says something profound about the man who rested there and those who loved him.

Then, finally, a lesson of hope. Because, in a tree above one of the graves, someone had hung an angel made out of netting. It was weathered and worn, but it endured.

And I realized again how that small cemetery held our greatest truths. How, whenever we worry about bills or the size of our house, we should drive to a cemetery. And how, there, the words "seize the day" seem to fill every rock, tree, and blade of grass.

Because in a cemetery, it all becomes clear. That everything we do today will pass. Except for the love.

for the children

I weep for the children. For their perfect faces and uncombed hair.

As a writer, I must tell you how it felt to hear about the murdered children in Littleton. As a man, I am speechless, wondering where it all went so wrong.

I first heard about the murders over the radio in a hardware store last week. The reports started slow, then came faster. With a quick nod to the owner, I realized that more children had been killed at school, this time in Colorado. But then, I continued looking for the paint I'd come for.

And that's what's so horrible about this. So disgusting. You see, it's actually becoming commonplace, these rampages! I almost took it in stride, that more kids had been killed. Ashamed to admit it, but it's true.

Days passed, and their pictures filled the television screen. Young faces who would never spend college nights sharing secrets with friends. Never get married. Never grow older or have children of their own whom they would hold in their arms and rock to sleep. All the dances they'd never dance, the dreams they'd never dream, the stars they'd never wish upon. All of it—gone.

Afterwards, I sat silent. Because it made no sense. Then, my thoughts went to my own children, almost asleep upstairs. In a near panic, I went up to Jeremy's room, wanting to teach him something quick so that he wouldn't one day be a face on the news. And, as I did, I thought of those Colorado parents who have only empty rooms to go to now.

At his door, I quietly called Jeremy's name. His sleepy "Huh?" came from the darkness.

"Bud," I whispered, "I want to talk to you. Is that okay?"

"Sure, Dad," he answered, waking more.

I knew I was about to have a conversation that I never thought I'd have. Such horrors I'd never hoped to see. I had to be careful, though, not to scare him.

"Jeremy," I began, as I sat down next to him on the bed. "What would you do if someone started shooting a gun at school?"

"Cool," he said, a little louder and a lot more interested. "Well, I'd dodge him like if he had a BB gun and try to take it away."

Dismay. Despair. For him, of course, it was a video game, a made-for-TV movie where people are shot and jump right back up. Images of the Colorado killing crashed into my brain, of gunmen (gunkids?) casually walking the school, searching.

"No!" I said. Probably louder than I needed to, but I was worried. "No, Jeremy, if someone starts shooting a gun, I want you to either run outside or get down on the floor."

"Okay," he said, obviously confused by my urgency.

So I reassured him and kissed him goodnight, hoping that I hadn't scared him too much but just enough.

Because I'm scared. In fact, I'm terrified. Because the children, our children, are dying, and I want it stopped. Right now. No ifs, ands, or buts. It's got to end.

Now, if I could just figure out where to start.

where there's a will

Gina and I are sitting in our lawyer's office. The clock might have moved but I'm not sure. Because I'm concentrating on the words.

"So, if you die, Jim, how will your family be provided for?"

I never knew words could cut so.

Die? Who the heck was planning on dying? I sure wasn't. No one had consulted me on this. No one had asked me if I planned to die, to leave my wife and my children.

But I guess every parent goes through this. The Grand Canyon of all questions. Because Gina and I had decided to do our wills and our lawyer was going through the possible scenarios.

"Okay, now, what if you're decapitated, Jim? How do you want to handle that?"

An image of just my head on a chair somewhere in the future trying to discipline my son. And him walking away with just the words "But, Dad, you're only a head! Ha! Ha!" over his shoulder.

"Gina, what if Jim dies? How would you want the money handled?"

An image of Gina and Mel Gibson jetting around the world spending millions of dollars. All right, so I'm not worth a million, but the movie rights to my life will probably bring something.

When did this madness start? When did I have to seriously consider my own death and not being there with my children on their wedding days?

So there we are, sitting with a lawyer talking about the day I wouldn't be there. The day I wouldn't come home to Matthew running up with his smile. The day that I wouldn't throw a baseball with Jeremy. The day I wouldn't kiss my so sweet daughter.

To not walk through a forest preserve, as my children mortared me with questions. Desperately searching back into my high school biology classes for the answers to why leaves change color and what side of the tree moss grows on.

To not be struck by my wife's beauty or the way she turns chocolate into little pieces of heaven.

These were the thoughts going through my brain as I came to terms with the legal terms for simply being gone.

questions

what have you grieved in your life?

did that grief change you?

what do you think your family and friends will say about you when you're gone?

what do you believe comes after death?

what three lessons do you most want to pass on?

part six

the search
for the
sacred you

≈

Simply
the thing that I am
shall make me live.
—William Shakespeare

are you who you wanted to be when you grew up? If so, what, then, is the content of your character and the format of your faith? And what makes up your sacred center, the part of you that doesn't change in the storm?

In this section, let's talk about you, about the incredible things you can do when you put your mind to it. When you are exactly who you are and do exactly what you were put here to do.

But, at the same time, let's also talk about the way we can drift through life, waiting on a savior to do it for us, although saviors are few and far between. And, when the only one who can define or confine you is standing in the mirror, which is hard metal to swallow. To know that we are responsible for what we become.

So, again, it comes back to a decision. Back to whether or not you have what it takes to take what the world has for you. Back to whether you'll ride the easy way out or burn your nose on the grindstone. The decision we make when everyone else is sleeping, the defining moments when we choose the path well traveled or the hills less pathed.

And, again I ask, are you who you wanted to be? Are you doing the things you hoped to be doing, loving the way you wanted to love, walking the roads you most needed to walk?

Or are you tired, worn down by the fight, and settling, instead, for a trip to the theater on Saturday night to see an actor playing the life you wanted? As he talks on the screen, so smooth in his scene, you mouth the words and fight to quiet your breaking heart.

Because it's so easy to go somewhere we never intended. And the scariest part of all is that losing ourselves doesn't happen all at once, illuminated by fireworks and the clash-bang of marching bands. Instead, we often forget our way slowly, over a matter of years.

So, to begin, I ask if you can hear your voice through the din of others' demands, through their wanting to help you be what they need you to be.

And, after drowning out their voices with your faith, when you finally find silence and push away the last jagged branches, will you find you waiting in the clearing? Where you're hoping to be led out into the light?

That's my wish for you, my friend. That's the act I hope you act. The most important decision you will ever make, to find yourself.

So here we go. But hold on tight and loose all at the same time—because this ride gets wacky and wild.

Fortunately, though, when it ends, you'll push up the bar, climb out of the car, and walk past the mirror. But as you do, you'll stop, retrace your steps, and stand in front of the glass. Where, after several moments, you'll smile.

You'll smile because you had become the person you always wanted to be. The true and sacred you.

what will i be?

When I was twelve, I remember wondering what I'd be doing in the year 2000.

In my bed on a late December night, with the snow kicking its tiny ice feet against my window, I thought, "Wow, in 2000, I'll be thirty-five! I wonder what I'll do then."

And, with my twelve-year-old brain, I thought about becoming a teacher, a doctor, or maybe an astronaut.

So, how has it turned out?

Well, I'm none of the above. But I've also learned that I was asking the wrong question. The question should have been, "*Who* will I be in the year 2000?"

Not what kind of job or title I'd have, but what would be my character, what would I believe in, and where would I take my stand and shout, "No further!"

And, today, looking in the only mirror I have—my heart—I see that I've now become a good man who tries to be true. A good man who most definitely has his weaknesses.

I say "tries" because, as you know, each path can be potholed with the darkest nights of the soul that we may ever know.

But, if I could, I'd go back and tell that twelve-year-old not to worry. Because, though I'm a million miles from perfect, I'll always try.

i wonder how you are

Although we may never have met, I hear your voice. Because the conviction of my words and the commitment of my flesh are that you and I are so much the same.

And I've been thinking and feeling about your stories, the ones you send me and the ones you may never send. The places you may be dancing or struggling through right now.

So, if you're happy, I wish you more. I wish you the utter abandon of love's sweet kiss.

But if there's something causing you pain, I wish you the gentlest hands of peace.

And if you feel alone, I can tell you that you're not. Because we're all here. And, although we may not know each other, we're still family.

Because like family, we care about each other and, sometimes, if the wind is just right, we can taste each other's tears.

And as family, we see the stories you bring when you visit, tucked carefully under your arm. We notice the way you jump at the sound of our hearts. And we understand how hard it can be.

So that's why we take your hand as we take your coat and lead you into the family room by the fire, where we ask you to sit and share your stories. And then we listen.

As it snows outside on a cold, cold night, we simply sit and listen.

snowflakes bearing gifts

I've learned to find meaning in ordinary moments. But each day, in the hurry of life, I often forget this lesson and need to learn it again. And, when I do, fortunately a teacher arrives.

Last Saturday, during the worst blizzard this city has seen in a long time, one that hit like a prizefighter, my teacher was a snowflake.

I knew the storm was different because, after waking, I looked out the window and couldn't see our patio. There'd been warnings, of course. The usual—that we would be receiving heavy snow. I just didn't realize that "heavy" meant more than fifteen inches. Obviously, whatever forces dictate how much snow will fall didn't take into account that I don't own a snowblower.

So there I stood, with the wind pounding the siding, knowing we'd probably be snowbound. I'd wanted to run errands and explore after-holiday sales. But it looked like Gina, Jeremy, Matthew, and I would be eating the day away, as all good snowbounders do.

But maybe, I thought, if I shoveled quickly enough, we could still get out. So I put on my thermal underwear, sweats, gloves, boots, and a coat, scarf, and facemask. I was ready.

As I walked toward the front door, I kissed Gina good-bye and told her that, if I didn't make it back from shoveling, she should marry again. Then I told her that I hoped she'd be happy. She just stood unblinking at my usual dramatics. The boys watched from the window, wondering why their dad needed so many clothes.

Outside, I contemplated the drifts. With the neighborhood frozen and nothing moving, I began shoveling. But the snow kept coming. The wind kept whipping. And my sound and fury was most definitely signifying nothing.

That's when I felt a tap on my shoulder. I looked around but found no one. Turning back to my work, though, I heard the voice.

"Jim," it beckoned, "over here!"

I turned to see a talking snowflake with two eyes and a beard.

Yes, I know what you're thinking. That the storm had frozen my brain into a cerebral Popsicle. But you would have been wrong. Because this snowflake was real, and it looked exactly like Abraham Lincoln. With a tall black hat, slightly askew from the wind.

"Uh, yeah," I answered, perplexed.

"Jim," the snowflake explained, "you've forgotten the lesson again. Forgotten why you're here, why we're all here."

"What are you talking about?" I asked, growing impatient. "I mean, come on. There's a brutal storm. My family's trapped and I'm freezing my face off talking to a snowflake. Now what the heck kind of lesson is that?"

"You know, Jim," he calmly answered. "It's about finding meaning in each day. And today, instead of finding the gift in this storm, you're angry and frantic." He was right.

I turned to my house. My wife and sons were watching me through the window, probably wondering whom I was talking to. And, at the same time, I realized that, because of the storm, we'd have at least a whole day to be together.

"Jim," the snowflake added, "don't you get it? It's all a gift. Doesn't it take you back to being a kid during a winter storm, when you hoped and prayed that they'd close the schools so you could grab your sled and run outside? Do you remember?"

I did. And thanked the snowflake, hugged him ever so gently, then watched him go. He turned once and waved. When he was gone, there was only silence.

With my lesson learned, I tilted my head to the sky and opened my mouth to catch snowflakes on my tongue, making sure all the while that they weren't wearing hats.

what's the buzz?

Tell me what's happening.

What's going on in your life? Where are you on the road to where you're going? Have you reached some or all of your goals? Are you happy? If you died today, would you be proud of what you've done so far?

Would you be willing to stand up for what you believe? Could there come a time when you give up everything you have for an ideal? Do you truly believe that "what goes around comes around"?

Has there ever been a time when your feet stopped moving, your hands stopped gesturing, your breathing eased, and you arrived at a moment where all you heard was the sunset and all you tasted was the sun?

If I asked you right now if you were being yourself and doing what you loved most, what would your answer be?

If I asked you right now if you still believed in magic, would you laugh and quickly walk away, mumbling to yourself that I'm a little strange?

Would you stop a meeting if someone said something you didn't believe, regardless of their title?

Where do you look for recognition? Work or home?

Where do you look to know that you are a success? Within or without?

Will you do one thing today to take one step closer to your dream?

Are you passionate about being alive, about having your feet attached to the mud of this brilliant blue ball that circles the sun?

And, of course, do you love?

just another save

"Every day, I find things to be thankful for. It's really wonderful," said Dan Quisenberry, former relief pitcher for the Kansas City Royals. "Sometimes, it's just seeing a little boy on a bicycle. Sometimes it's the taste of water. It's hard to explain."*

These were Dan Quisenberry's words in January of 1998, after he had gone through a surgery in which doctors removed most of a severe brain tumor. Most.

As a pitcher, Quisenberry ranked high on baseball's all-time saves list. But it wasn't his accomplishments on the field that amazed me. It was the fact that this man, facing death, said that life was "wonderful."

In the suffering, he found gifts. In the darkness, he found light. And Dan Quisenberry died at the age of forty-five.

So let's not wait to begin to live. And let's not take one more day for granted. Let's remember, instead, that it's good just to talk to a friend or wave to a child.

And let's keep moving through these breaths. Let's not let one more day go by without telling everyone we love that we love them. Without showing others that we'd walk through fire just to tell them we care. And let's not hold on to the hate if there's a way, any way, to let it go.

Let's do all this in memory of Dan who, after learning that he was dying, took the time to notice a boy on a bike and the simple gift of water. Because, if we're not careful, we may never see.

Good-bye, Dan. And God speed.

* *Chicago Tribune*, 1998.

it's a wonder full life

Once upon a time, George Bailey forgot what he meant to others. But, with the help of an angel's hands, he realized that no one knows "how many lives one life touches."

And I was wondering if you know how many lives your life has touched.

Whether it was that morning last summer when you stopped to give directions to that older man who'd lost his way. Or that night in March when you volunteered at the children's hospital.

Or how about the time you noticed your co-worker crying and, instead of running to your meeting, you pulled up a chair and pulled out her story.

Even in the quieter moments, you changed lives. When my father died and you sent me cards, saying my family was in your thoughts. Well, I took those cards to my mom at the funeral. As she read them, she cried, knowing you cared.

And do you understand? Do you realize that nothing would be the same without you? The snow may fall differently. The trees might grow upside down. And somewhere there'd be a hole where your laughter should be.

So, learn again that you are irreplaceable. That you are something gentle set upon this world to bring hope where there's despair, faith where there's doubt, and love where there's someone sitting alone at their kitchen table wondering when the phone will ring.

It's a wonderful life, my friend. Because of you.

"take your inner child to work" day

I didn't believe our company's "Take Your Inner Child to Work" Day would really happen . . . until I saw it.

I walked into the department to find Joan and Katie, my co-workers, running through the cubes, playing tag. Meanwhile, Harry, my usually conservative colleague, was drawing hopscotch lines in the hall. Farther down, Bill made paper airplanes.

In other departments, people stood in wonder, looking out at the new baby geese in the courtyard. And the familiar became extraordinary. For instance, I can't tell you how many employees simply stood by the copier, amazed at how it collated.

Some people didn't make it in to work until later. They had awakened on time, but stayed home to watch "Dora the Explorer" and "Blues Clues" before putting on their mismatched clothes and dirtied Keds. Then, before leaving for work, they packed a bag of Cheerios and Goldfish Crackers for snack time.

But later, when we got down to business, productivity soared. Because, like children, people were creative and all said what they felt. In meetings, if an idea was presented that didn't yet make sense, someone would say, "Hey, that idea doesn't yet make sense." However, if the idea was a good one, high fives were exchanged all around and a break was taken to play the latest Nintendo game.

It was also rumored that somewhere in a corporate classroom, a presenter looked up from her notes, smiled, and declared that it was time for recess. Executives loved the monkey bars. A handful of managers waited for the swings.

In the afternoon, employees pulled out their rugs from desk drawers and took a nap. Afterwards, it was time for cookies and a story: something from the annual report, I think.

As for me, I learned something important on "Take Your Inner Child to Work" Day. I learned that we're all still seven years old inside. And that those seven-year-olds can be demanding, pounding on our chests, wanting to be let out once in awhile.

So I let mine out a little more every day. The hard part is getting him back in.

try again

My youngest son, Matthew, uses these words whenever he attempts something that doesn't work out at first. Whether it's getting his zipper jammed or not catching a ball, he simply says, "Try again" and has another go at it.

And, once again, the child is father of the man, for he has taught me well.

After all, it's easy to stop trying, whether it's out of fear, despair, or just being tired. But kids keep going. They usually don't give up or in or any of the other countless ways we learn to turn away from what we want.

So I've been learning to not believe that every falling down will be my downfall. To not see defeat before the battle's begun.

And if, on some Monday, it crosses your mind to not try, to simply settle, I'd ask you to remember a little boy. One who looks at failure as just another chance to show what he's made of.

do you know how powerful you are?

Do you realize that you could tear open the skies with your hands?

Do you know that your feet can cut rivers across the earth?

Or do you still believe in the lie that you are merely someone who does what they're told?

Do you understand that comets would bow before you if you'd only take your rightful place among the heavens?

Do you comprehend the magic that curls beneath the swirls of your fingertips?

Or will you simply turn the page?

Well, you know, I was born to bug you, to find some endless way to drive you mad until you yell, "Stop!"

Because in that yelling, in that action, in that doing something, in that moment with no hesitation, in that rage to stand and fight, therein lies the secret.

The secret of how powerful you really are . . .

Now, how will you use that power today?

in the giving

They say it's better to give than receive. But receiving can be pretty tough, too.

I have a hard time letting people take care of me. Mostly because, when they do, my first thought is usually, "Am I really worth this?"

But then I counter with another thought. "Yes, of course, I'm worth it. We're all worth it. After all, isn't it me who always says we're loved? Well, being loved means you're worth it."

Afterwards, when I'm not so caught up in the fight my thoughts fought, I realize once again what it is we have to do to be worthy of love.

Absolutely nothing. That's right. Not a darn thing. Because we're worth it right now, as is, where we stand, take it or take it.

You're worth love and I'm worth love. And always the twain shall meet.

Now, of course, being worthy makes its demands. Because the moment we know we're loved just because we're who we are is the moment we see each other that way, too. And then we must decide whether or not to act on our new sight.

Whether it's helping a despairing man stand. Or making a shelter a home to the weary and battered. Or simply stopping on the way to the kitchen to tell your daughter she's your sugar dumpling. All of it, giving to others gives right back to us in the joy of touching lives.

So, today, we'll receive. And tomorrow we'll give. And, if we do it right, we won't be able to tell the difference.

the toughest days

These are the toughest days. As the alarm goes off and the day goes on.

On the way to work, then, thinking about you. About what I wanted to share with you today.

And all I want to talk about is how hard it can be to get started on some days, the ones that are darkly the same and filled with things we have to do. When all we really want to do is stay in bed, pull the covers up around our shoulders, and dream on.

But in my car, on the dashboard, there's a note with two questions on it that caught my eye as it always does. Two questions a friend asked me when I said that I wanted to fulfill my purpose, to be who I am, to do what I feel that I was put here to do.

"Do you want it?" and "How badly do you want it?"

My answers:

"Yes" and "Badly."

So, today, on this morning like so many others, when I'd rather do anything but do anything, I will once again move. Because wanting it badly doesn't mean anything if I don't do something about it.

After all, the world's filled with people who wanted it badly. But people who can change the world with their blistered hands are pretty rare.

But they're out there. Are you one of them?

eighteen seconds

For eighteen seconds, think about who you love.

For seventeen seconds, remember how you are blessed.

For sixteen seconds, dance like the leaves.

For fifteen seconds, try not to smile.

For fourteen seconds, listen to time and what it's trying to tell you.

For thirteen seconds, believe in Willy Wonka.

For twelve seconds, walk into the fear.

For eleven seconds, think about the people who've touched your heart.

For ten seconds, become a child again.

For nine seconds, think about the people in your life who are difficult, and then figure out how they might have gotten that way.

For eight seconds, feel the solar system turning inside you.

For seven seconds, think about where you'd like to go one day . . . then plan how to get there.

For six seconds, pretend that you can fly.

For five seconds, remember the best moment of your life and dedicate yourself to making even better ones.

For four seconds, let it all go.

For three seconds, dream in black and white with just a dash of honeysuckle red.

For two seconds, count the holes in the ceiling.

For one second, realize that it's all precious.

Then start all over again.

did you touch
the world's skin?

Did you touch the world's skin this week?

Or was it easier to ease through, carefully avoiding souls and sidewalk cracks?

Did you make a difference in the weave of someone's heart?

Or was it smoother to just walk away, hoping they didn't hear you?

Did you inch closer to the person you long to be?

Or were you silenced by the thought of being vulnerable?

Did you teach courage to another?

Or was it less trouble to drop down on the couch and catch a ballgame?

And if you moved the world last week, then what will you do for an encore?

And if you didn't, what will it take to make you move?

To help you understand that you hold the power to do anything, to be anyone, to tear the stars from the night and factor them into your life.

What will it take to make you believe that you belong, that you are worthy, that you are perfect the way you are?

Do you believe?

Do you believe?

Do you believe?

And, most red and white and true of all, do you love?

we can do great things

We can do great things. But first, we have to commit. Commit to moving, not hiding. To coming out of the shadows and into the light, where we can be seen.

Because we have a responsibility, you and I. A responsibility to leave someone or something better. To make something happen instead of waiting for someone to do it for us.

For, if we don't commit to this slice of the world our feet are stuck to, nothing will change. We'll simply go through life like ghosts.

So, what if you and I do one thing this week to make something or someone better, including ourselves? What would you do? When would you start? What stands in your way? And how will you feel when you've done it?

We can do great things. Isn't it about time we started?

you're amazing

Just when I think I've got you pegged, you go and do something that makes me think even more of you. Like your stories about loving people back into the light who had somehow found themselves alone in the dark. Like your persistence in pursuit of a dream, of your purpose for being. Or the fact that even though you've suffered through the highest slice of pain, you refuse to give up.

You just amaze me.

And I hope I don't embarrass you by telling you that I'm proud of you, or that I wish I had more of your strength. In fact, sometimes, I wish I had even a fragment of your faith.

Because you walk so tall and move so quickly through the lies that keep me sucked thigh-deep in the mud.

So you're amazing.

Now, I know you don't really want to hear this. And I know you're too humble to believe half of what I'm saying. But I also know that I've been watching you and the way you take on the world but still find time to play Candyland with the kids or call your mom or simply find a home for a dog.

And, again, I have to say that you inspire me. Breathe life and purpose into my walk and power and passion into my words with your very presence.

So be still, my friend, and know that you've touched me, and left me changed.

You're amazing. And I just thought you should know.

it's time

It's time to get a little crazy.

It's time to not play it safe.

It's time to love again, no matter what scars your heart holds.

It's time to believe, despite the fact that the last time you did, you ended up betrayed.

It's time to stand upon the feet you were given and find some peace in the rain.

It's time.

It's time to move.

It's time to risk again, to walk into fear with nothing but a pocketful of faith and your steely, steely eyes.

It's time to tell yourself that you belong, so what's all the fuss about.

It's time to fly, although your wings are wet.

It's time.

It's time to update your resume with a line about how great you do the thing you do that you were put here to do when you do it.

It's time to finally understand that everything is within your reach if you'll just stick out your hand.

It's time to show us how to make it better.

It's time.

It's really, truly, simply, bluely time.

So, if it is, and if we know exactly what we need to do to get started, what's stopping us?

Is it fear?

Or is it the tangy taste of anticipation?
No matter, because we have a responsibility, you and I.
To begin.
And there's no time like the present.
Because it's time.

a man for others

When my brother and I were young, my dad would wake us up each Saturday morning during the summer, load the lawnmower into the car, and drive us to St. Ephrem's, our church. There we'd mow the lawn, trim the bushes, clean up the grounds, laugh and sweat, and just enjoy being with Dad. It is one of the finest memories I have.

We could have been home playing. And my dad could have been relaxing after a hard week of work and night school. But we weren't. Because my dad loved his community and wanted to serve. And he wanted us to learn to do the same.

Then there were the nights spent listening to him talk about the war. Of how scared he was as a young man to be facing death. But also, how that fear could never equal the responsibility he felt to serve because of the love he had for those who fought at his side, for his country, and for the people he was trying to save. It stays with me still.

Then, last week, my mother's sister died, and her funeral was at St. Ephrem's. Watching my mother struggle with the loss of her sister so soon after the loss of her husband was fire on my skin.

But, in the months before, my mom had spent time caring for her sister, visiting her through snowstorms and her own grieving. Because she loved her sister and wanted to serve.

After the funeral, sitting in the van with Gina, I looked at the yard we used to mow, amazed at how small it had become, forgetting for a moment how everything shrinks when we grow. But, at the same time, I also remembered how it felt to serve.

And it came to me that the only reason we're here is to serve, to help others, and to let each soul we meet along the way know they're loved.

Dad, I think I've got it.

questions

what were you put here to do?

if you haven't done it, when will you start?

how would your best friend describe you to a person who doesn't know you?

when do you stop to take stock of your life and what you're doing with it?

why are you amazing?

part seven

hearing your
small, small
voice

~

One man scorned
and covered with scars
still strove with his
last ounce of courage
to reach the unreachable stars;
and the world will be
better for this.
—Cervantes,
"The Impossible Dream"

where are we going so fast?

The question first came to me in a small, small voice.

It came a few years ago in a period of suffering, a time when I left much of what I knew to become a stranger in an estranged land.

But, in that new place, where I didn't fit and could hardly breathe, I realized what I was here for. And, woven there, within the pain of leaving friends and so much behind, was the gift. And that voice.

The one that said, "Tell them that they're not alone so they needn't be afraid. Tell them that I've hidden sacred lessons within their moments to show them that they are connected to each other, and to me. And most of all, tell them that they are loved."

Now, as many people would do in that situation, I questioned what I'd heard and, finding no real evidence of the voice or where it came from, dismissed it. But dismissing a voice that comes from within is like killing crabgrass. Not an easy task, even when you've got the right tools.

And I definitely had what I thought were the right tools. I had my logic. I had my reasons for all the reasons I didn't believe in voices. I had my plans and patterns laid out end to end, to the point where the whole world was nothing but a problem to be solved.

Until that voice.

Each day it came, growing louder and more demanding. And, along the way, I kept meeting people who heard their own voice, with a message all their own but mysteriously the same.

The real challenge, though, was that once I accepted the message, I became responsible for sharing it. Responsible for asking where we're going so fast when all that matters is already there, clinging to the edges of our day with weakening fingers, hoping we'll notice it before it falls. Responsible for figuring out, once and for all, if I really believe in something behind the something I see.

So, today, after years of struggling to share the words, I've come to realize that the voice was me and you and

God and the trees and the stars and the upper half of the lower half of the world and everything in between, asking me to share the lessons I most need to learn.

And I wonder if you hear your small, small voice. One similar in sound but most likely with a message meant only for you.

Have you found what you were put here to do, your divine purpose for being? If not, how will you begin to listen? How will you quiet your brain enough to hear the words that tell you your truth and nothing but your truth?

Will it be today? And, if not, when? Because what could be more important than listening for a voice that voices your purpose? What could be more important than using each day to move along your path when we're here for such a short time?

Where are we going so fast?

Nowhere. Because if we just walk this path without feeling the stones through our shoes, without finding our voice, and without feeling the wind against our cheeks and the hand holding ours, then we have no real destination and we're just passing time.

I wish you peace, my friend. I wish you love. And, most of all, I wish you the quiet and blessings to hear your small, small voice.

did you ever forget
who you were?

We went to a neighbor's party this weekend. Remembering that he played music, it came as little surprise that there was a variety of musical instruments throughout the house. What did come as a surprise was how sad I felt seeing them.

You see, I love music. I always have. In fact, I played guitar professionally when I was younger, so much younger than today, in bands throughout Chicago. Our glory day, as Bruce would say, was opening one night for Bob Marley's Wailers.

But, sadly, I haven't played in quite awhile. I always say I will, when I have more time. However, more time will probably come around the month of Never.

Which is a shame. Because music is as much a part of me as writing. In fact, it's one of the loves I shared with my dad. Plus, by not playing, I'm not passing that love on to my children.

And I know they'd like it, because I finally picked up a guitar at my neighbor's party and played for them. At first, with fumbling fingers, then, smoother, funkier, and bluesier, as it came back to me how much I needed music. And how easy it is to lose track of ourselves in the day-to-day race for first place.

So, I'll bring music back into our house. Because my family deserves my passion. And because it's harder to get where you're going when you forget parts of yourself along the way.

questions

when you look back at your life, what moment are you proudest of?

have you learned your greatest lessons in joy or suffering?

have you ever taken the time to hear your small, small voice?

if you have, what has it told you?

if you haven't, when will you?

afterword

I'd love to hear about your special moments and your comments about this book. If you do send in a moment, please also send your contact information. Then, you and I may be able to work together to share your story in a future book.

Please write or e-mail your stories and comments to me at either of the addresses below. Also, you can learn more about my workshops and speaking. Perhaps we will have the chance to meet someday.

Mail:

Jim Warda c/o Sheed & Ward, 7373 South Lovers Lane Road, Franklin, Wisconsin 53132.

E-mail:

Wordwind5@aol.com

Also, you can subscribe to my free weekly online column, "Moments Online." Simply send an e-mail with "Subscribe" in the Subject box to Wordwind5@aol.com.

Take care, my friend

—Jim Warda

acknowledgments

So many people create a writer that it doesn't seem fair to put just one name on the cover. But, since the cover's only so big, I need to say "Thank you" to:

Gina, who believed in me even when I didn't believe in myself. I never knew . . .

Jeremy, Matthew, and Alexandra. Before them, I simply had words. With them, I have something to say.

My mother, Hannah, who keeps everything I've ever written in a binder. Every writer needs someone like that. So, does every son.

My sister, Bobbie, brothers, Geoff and Greg, and their husband, wives, and children. And, Gina's parents, Leo and June Lento. They are blessings upon me.

Jeremy Langford, my editor, and Joe Durepos, my literary agent, who gave me a chance. There are few greater gifts.

Kathleen Kikkert, who took my message and captured it in the cover of this book.

And, for everyone else who has helped me along the way, including Jack Canfield, who was so kind in writing the Foreword, Patty Aubery and the Chicken Soup staff; Kass Dotterweich; Barbara Glanz; Stephen Hrycyniak; Phil Kirschbaum; Kathleen Phillips; Rae Potter; Bob Redman; Gail Reichlin; Johnny Shumate; Michael Smith; Al Gustafson, Robyn Johnson, and Mary Beth Sammons of *The Works* magazine; and Denise Joyce and Marla Krause at the *Chicago Tribune*. If I missed anyone, I apologize.

Then, for the writers, including James Autry, William Faulkner, Natalie Goldberg, Ernest Hemingway, Laurie Beth Jones, John Keats, Stephen King, Gregg Levoy, and William Shakespeare. In watching them work their craft, I learned mine.

Finally, for my readers. Together, we make it sacred. And for you, one final gift:

> There is but one rule of conduct for a man—to do the right thing. The cost may be dear in money, in friends, in influence, in labor, in a prolonged and painful sacrifice; but the cost not to do right is far more dear: you pay in the integrity of your manhood, in honor, in truth, in character. You forfeit your soul's content, and for a timely gain you barter the infinities.
>
> —Archer G. Jones